English
At Your Command!

HAMPTON-BROWN

Copyright © Hampton – Brown

All rights reserved. No part of this book may be reproduced or transmitted in any form or by any means, electronic or mechanical, including photocopying, recording, or by any information storage and retrieval system, without permission in writing from the publisher.

Hampton – Brown
P.O. Box 223220
Carmel, California 93922
800-333-3510
www.hampton-brown.com

Printed in the United States of America

ISBN 0-7362-1646-4   Softcover
ISBN 0-7362-1645-6   Hardcover

03 04 05 06 07 08 09 10 11 12 9 8 7 6 5 4 3 2 1

Hampton-Brown extends special thanks to the following consultants who contributed to the development of *English At Your Command!*

Sue Goldstein
Bilingual Team Leader / Grade 3 Teacher
Puentes Two-Way Bilingual Program
Regional Multicultural Magnet School
New London, Connecticut

Lizabeth Lepovitz
Bilingual Teacher, Grades 2, 3
J. L. Carson Elementary School
Northside ISD
San Antonio, Texas

Raul C. Ramirez, Jr.
Grade 3 Bilingual / Gifted and Talented Teacher
Royalgate Elementary School
South San Antonio ISD
San Antonio, Texas

Ruth Woods
ESL Teacher, Grades 2, 3, 4, 5
Minneapolis Public Schools
Minneapolis, Minnesota

Acknowledgments

Every effort has been made to secure permission, but if any omissions have been made, please let us know. We gratefully acknowledge permission to reprint the following material:

P3, p13 and p295: "Getting About – Flyers" from *Bugs* by Gerald Legg. Copyright © 1998 Quadrillion Publishing, Ltd. Used by permission of Chrysalis Books, Ltd., London.

P103 and p219: *Two of Everything* by Lily Toy Hong. Copyright © 1993 by Lily Toy Hong. Reprinted by permission of Albert Whitman Company. All rights reserved.

P123: *Dear Juno* cover from *Dear Juno* by Soyung Pak, illustrated by Susan Kathleen Hartung. Copyright © 1999 by Susan Kathleen Hartung, illustrations. Used by permission of Viking Penguin, an imprint of Penguin Putnam Books for Young Readers, a division of Penguin Putnam, Inc. All rights reserved.

Pp144–145: Elements of the play *Annie*, by Thomas Meehan. Used by permission of the author.

P146: "Rainy Day" by William Wise from *All On a Summer Day* published by Pantheon. Copyright © 1971 by William Wise. Reprinted by permission of Curtis Brown, Ltd.

P147: "Tommy" by Gwendolyn Brooks from *Bronzeville Boys and Girls*. Copyright © 1956 by Gwendolyn Brooks Blakely. Used by permission of HarperCollins Publishers.

P148: "There Was a Young Lady " from *The Complete Nonsense of Edward Lear*. Copyright © 1951, Dover Publications, Inc. Used by permission of the publisher.

P149: "Ears Hear" by Hymes Jr., James and Lucia, from *Oodles of Noodles*. Copyright © 1964. Reprinted by permission of Pearson Education, Inc.

P182 and p188: From *Too Many Tamales* by Gary Soto, illustrated by Ed Martinez. Copyright © 1993 by Ed Martinez, illustrations. Used by permission of G.P. Putnam's Sons, an imprint of Penguin Putnam Books for Young Readers, a division of Penguin Putnam Inc. All rights reserved.

P183: Image from p23 *Lon Po Po* by Ed Young. Copyright © 1989 by Ed Young. Used by permission of Philomel Books, an imprint of Penguin Putnam Books for Young Readers, a division of Penguin Putnam Inc. All rights reserved.

P231: Facsimile page from Primary Dictionary. Copyright © 1991 Macmillan/McGraw-Hill Publishing Company. Used by permission of The McGraw-Hill Companies.

P281: "Ice Skating" by Sandra Liatsos. Copyright © 1982 by Sandra Liatsos. Used by permission of Marian Reiner.

Pp297–298 and pp300–301: *The Honey Makers* copyright © 1997 by Gail Gibbons. Used by permission of HarperCollins Publishers.

Pp297–298: Cover art from *The Life and Times of the Honeybee*. Copyright © 1995 by Charles Micucci. Used by permission of Houghton Mifflin Company. All rights reserved.

P297 and p299: Larry West, *Ranger Rick* August 1996 cover (bee). From *Ranger Rick*, used by permission of photographer.

P299: Reprinted with the permission of Simon & Schuster Books for Young Readers, an imprint of Simon & Schuster Children's Publishing Division from *Macmillan Dictionary for Children*, revised by Robert B. Costello, Editor in Chief. Copyright © 1997 Simon & Schuster.

P299 and p316: From *The World Book Encyclopedia*. Copyright © 1998 World Book, Inc. By permission of the publisher. www.worldbook.com

P317: Facsimile page from *The World Book Student Discovery Encyclopedia*. Copyright © 2002 World Book, Inc. By permission of the publisher.

P319: Tom Leeson, *Ranger Rick* January 2002 cover (coyote). From *Ranger Rick*, used by permission of the photographer.

Photography:

P32 and p33: Courtesy of the Aceves family (grandparents).

P144: Courtesy of the Fredericksburg Theatre Company, Mary Washington College, Dept. of Theatre and Dance, Fredericksburg, VA (Annie).

Animals Animals/Earth Scenes: p75 (slow turtle, © Robert Winslow), p131 (bird © Ron Willocks; fox, © Robert Maier).

Acknowledgments continued on pages 351-352.

Welcome!

In this book, you will find all kinds of ways to **communicate**. When you communicate, you say what you are thinking, feeling, and imagining. This book will help you find the words you need. It will show you how English works. You will learn how to organize your ideas and write about them. You will even learn how to do research in the library and on the Internet, too!

Whenever you have a question about English, you can look here first. This book will put **English At Your Command!**

Table of Contents

Chapter 1
Just the Right Word 14

Words About You 16
- Actions 18
- Feelings 19
- Colors 20
- Shapes 21
- Sizes 22
- Sounds 23
- Smells 24
- Touch 25
- Tastes 26
- At Home 28
- Family 32

Words About Your School 34
- Inside the School 36
- People at School 38
- In a Classroom 40
- Things to Do 42
- Numbers 44
- Number Order 47
- Say Hello 48
- Say Good-bye 49
- Say Thank You 50
- Meet New People 51
- Ask for Help 52

Words About Your World 54
In Your Community 56
Community Workers 58
Doctor's Office 60
Transportation 62
Signs and Safety 64
Time
Days of the Week 66
Months and Seasons 67
Telling Time 68
Weather 70

Words! Words! Words! 72
Synonyms 72
Antonyms 74
Compound Words 76
Suffixes 78
Prefixes 79
Multiple-Meaning Words 80
Sound-Alike Words 82

Chapter 2
Picture It! 84
Charts 86
  KWL Chart 87
Clusters
  Web 88
  Character Map 89
Diagrams
  Parts Diagram 90
  Process Diagram 91
  Venn Diagram 92
  Main Idea Diagram 93

Graphs
    Bar Graph 94
    Line Graph 95
    Pie Graph 96

Map 97

Story Maps
    Character, Setting, and Plot 98
    Beginning, Middle, and End 99
    Sequence Chain 100
    Problem-and-Solution Map 101
    Goal-and-Outcome Map 102
    Cause-and-Effect Map 103

Time Lines 104

Chapter 3
Put It in Writing! 106
The Writing Process 108
Kinds of Writing

Announcement 122
Book Review 123
Description
   Description of a Person 124
   Description of a Place 125
Directions
   How to Make Something 126
   How to Get to a Place 127
E-mail 128
Fable 129
Journal Entry 130
Labels and Captions 131
Letters and Notes
   Friendly letter 132
   Envelope 133
   Invitation 134
   Thank-you Note 135
   Postcard 136
List 137
Message 137
Newsletter
   News Story 138
   Advertisement 139

Paragraph
   A Paragraph with Examples 140
   Sequence Paragraph. 141
   A Paragraph That Compares. 142
   Opinion Paragraph 143

Play 144

Poem
   Rhyming Poem 146
   Limerick 148
   Poem with Sound Words 149

Story 150
   Realistic Fiction. 151
   Fantasy 152

A Story About You 154

Summary 156

The Good Writer Guide

How to Collect Ideas 158
How to Write for a Purpose. 160
Choose a Form for Your Purpose 164
How to Write for Your Audience 166
How to Choose Words
   Use Precise Words 168
   Use Vivid Words 169
How to Use a Thesaurus 170
How to Write Better Sentences
   Write Complete Sentences 172
   Combine Short Sentences. 173
   Fix Run-on Sentences. 174
   Use Different Kinds of Sentences 175
How to Add Details 176
Show, Don't Tell. 177
Review Your Writing 178

Chapter 4
Present It! 180

- **Read Aloud** 182
- **Listen to a Story** 183
- **Give a Message** 184
- **Get a Message** 185
- **Give a Talk** 186
- **Listen to a Talk** 187
- **Talk in a Group** 188
- **Listen in a Group** 189
- **Find and Make Pictures** 190
- **View Pictures** 192

Handwriting and Spelling Guide

Get Ready to Write 194
Manuscript Alphabet 195
   Write Letters 196
   Write Words and Sentences 197
   Write Sentences in a Paragraph 198
Cursive Alphabet 199
   Write Words 200
   Write Sentences 201
   Write Sentences in a Paragraph 202
Spell Sounds in English
   Spell Consonant Sounds 204
   Spell Short Vowel Sounds 210
   Spell One Sound with Two Letters 211
   Spell Two Sounds with Two Letters 212
   Spell Long Vowels 214
   Spell Words with *c* and *g* 216
   Spell Words with Vowel + *r* 217
   Spell More Vowel Sounds 218
   Spell Words with *–ed, -ing, -er, –est* 220
   Spell Plurals 222
   Spell Long Words 223
Spell These Right!
   Words That Sound Alike 224
   Words That Kids Misspell 226
Spelling Tips 228
Use a Dictionary 230

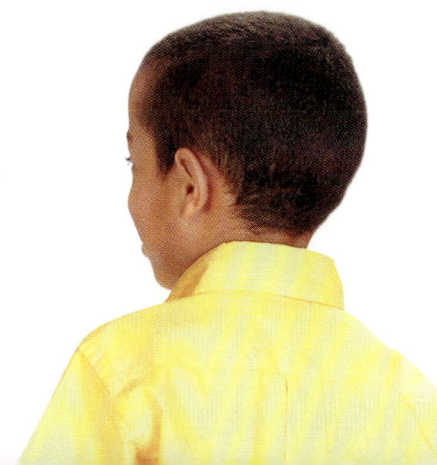

Chapter 5
Grammar Made Graphic 232

- Sentences 234
- Negative Sentences 237
- Complete Sentences 238
- Longer Sentences 239
- Write Sentences 241
- Common Nouns 242
- Proper Nouns 245
- More than One 246
- *A*, *An*, and *The* 248
- Possessive Nouns 250
- Use Nouns in Writing 251
- Pronouns 252
- *This*, *That*, *These*, *Those* 260
- Use Pronouns in Writing 261
- Adjectives 262
- Adjectives That Compare 264
- Adjectives in Sentences 266
- Use Adjectives in Writing 267
- Action Verbs 268
- The Verbs *Am*, *Is*, and *Are* 270
- The Verbs *Has* and *Have* 271
- Actions in the Present 272
- Actions in the Past 273
- Actions in the Future 276
- Helping Verbs 278
- Use Verbs in Writing 281
- Adverbs 282
- Use Adverbs in Writing 283
- Capital Letters 284
- Punctuation Marks 288

Chapter 6
Look It Up! 294

The Research Process 296
Research Tools
Books 312
Encyclopedia 316
Experts 318
Magazines 319
Internet 320

Grammar Practice 322

Index 346

Where do you live?
What is the weather like?
What do you like to do?

You can tell about anything with just the right word.

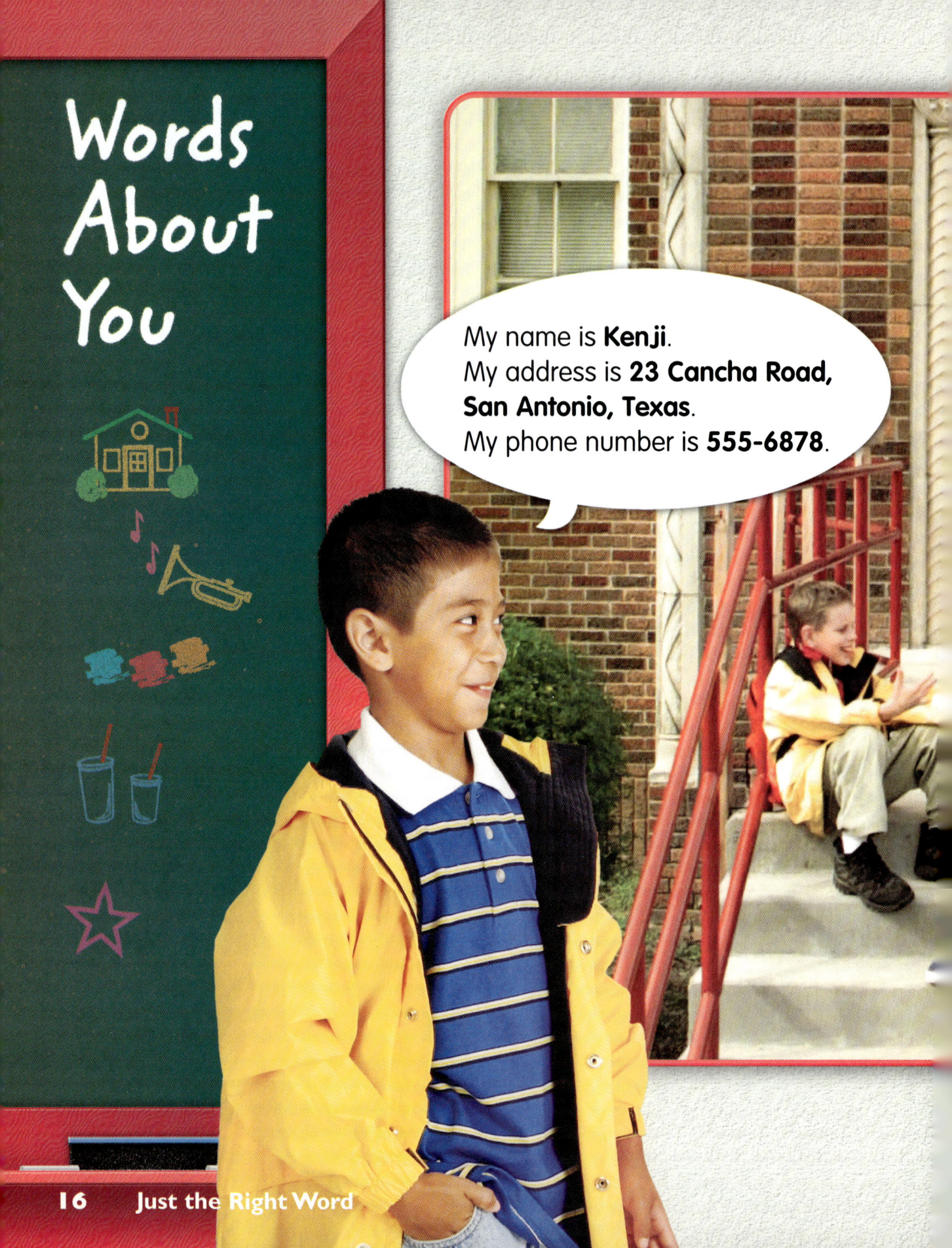

Actions

I can **read**.

I can **eat**.

I can **paint**.

I can **run**.
What can you do?

I can **write**.

I can **carry**.

Just the Right Word

Feelings

I am **confused**.

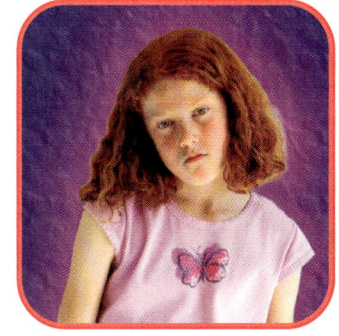
I am **sad**.

I am **surprised**.

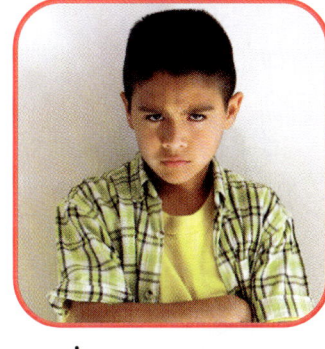
I am **angry**.

I am **bored**.

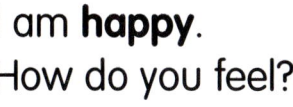
I am **happy**. How do you feel?

Colors

white

purple

brown

yellow

red

pink

orange

gold

green

blue

black

gray

I like **blue**.
What color do you like?

Shapes

circle oval square

rectangle triangle star

I have a **red circle**. What do you have?

Sizes

Just the Right Word

Sounds

quiet whisper

noisy drum

I hear a **loud** horn. What do you hear?

Smells

sweet flower

clean towel

rotten garbage

fresh bread

I smell a **stinky** sock. What do you smell?

24 Just the Right Word

Touch

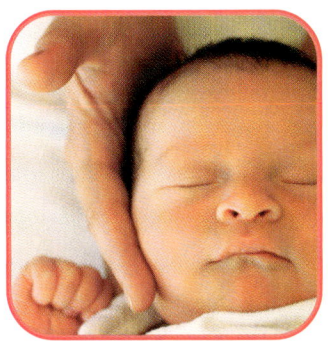
smooth skin

soft pillow

wet hair

hot drink

I feel a **bumpy** pineapple. What do you feel?

Tastes

sweet cake

spicy salsa

salty pretzel

tangy orange

I taste a **sour** lemon.

At Home

window
gate

apartment building

mobile home

town house

Just the Right Word

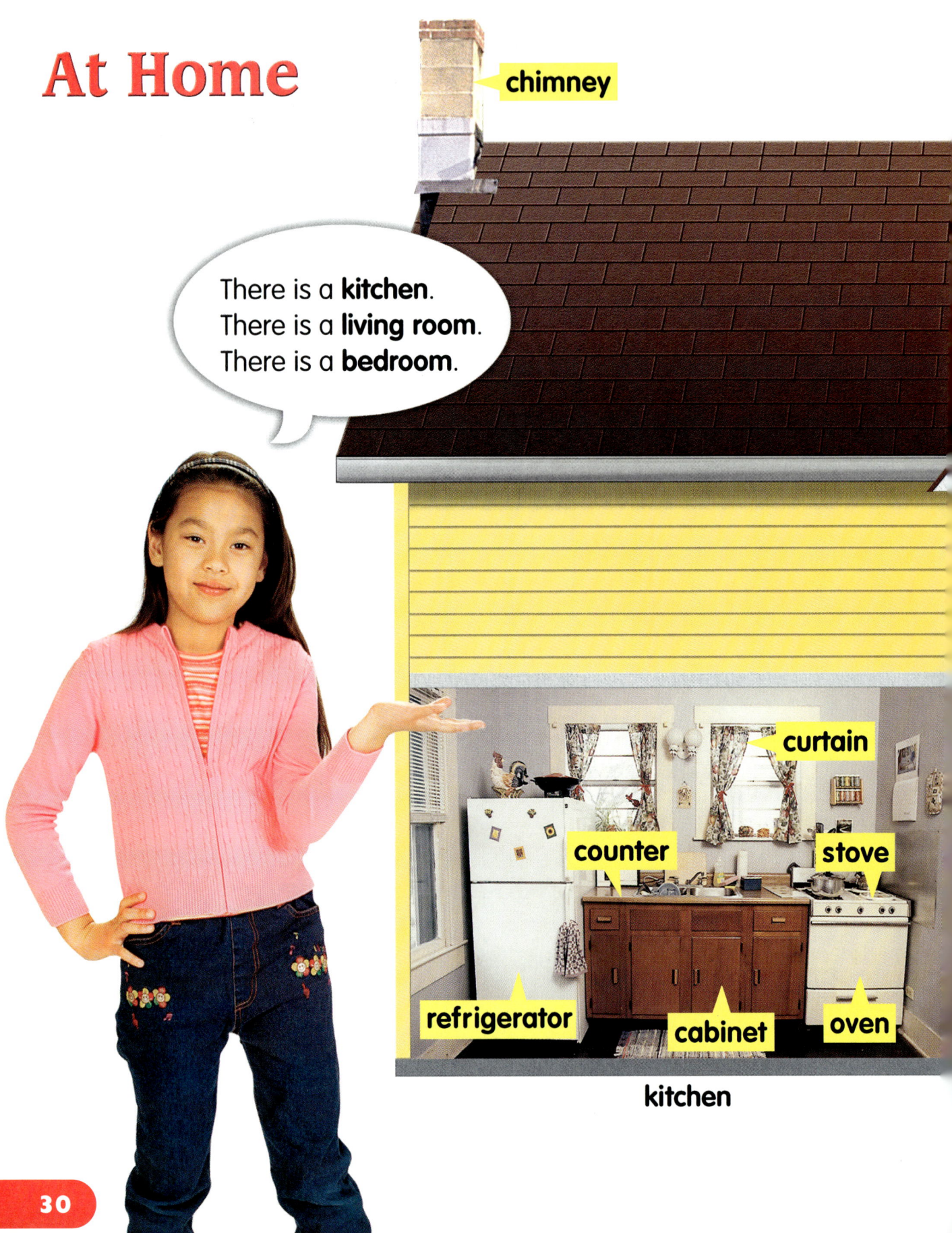

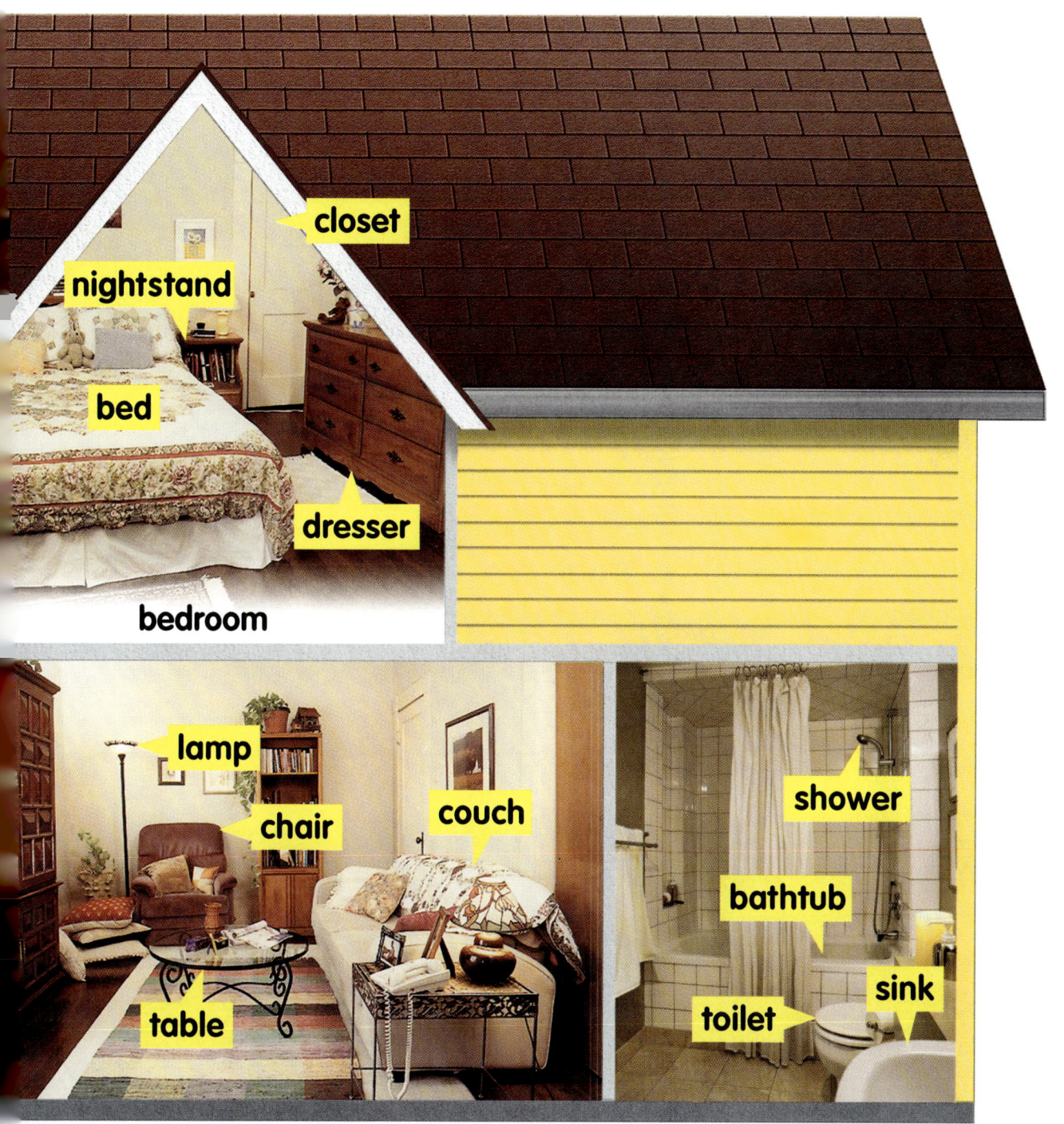

Family

Just the Right Word!

Inside the School

Just the Right Word

library

office

girls' bathroom

cafeteria

Just the Right Word

People at School

The **teacher** teaches a student.

The **students** write.

The **librarian** finds books.

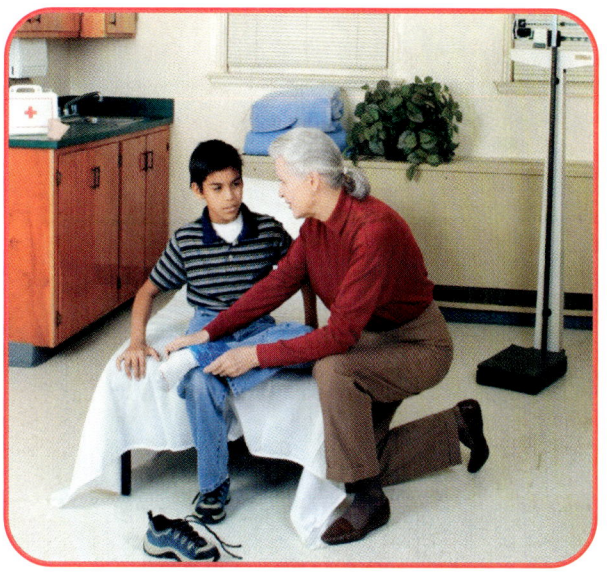
The **nurse** helps sick and hurt people.

The **custodian** cleans the school.

The **principal** leads the school.

Who works in your school?

In a Classroom

This is my **classroom**.
Here is a **teacher**.
Here are some **students**.

student

pencil

crayon

chalk

ruler

scissors

eraser

glue

Just the Right Word

Things to Do

Circle the correct picture.

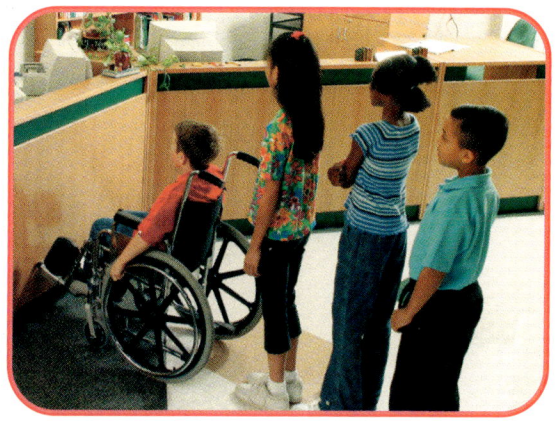
Line up.

Put an X on the square.

Sit down.

Stand up.

Numbers

1 one
2 two
3 three
4 four
5 five
6 six
7 seven
8 eight
9 nine
10 ten

I have **five** buttons in each group.

More than 10

11	eleven	21	twenty-one	40	forty
12	twelve	22	twenty-two	50	fifty
13	thirteen	23	twenty-three	60	sixty
14	fourteen	24	twenty-four	70	seventy
15	fifteen	25	twenty-five	80	eighty
16	sixteen	26	twenty-six	90	ninety
17	seventeen	27	twenty-seven	100	one hundred
18	eighteen	28	twenty-eight	1,000	one thousand
19	nineteen	29	twenty-nine		
20	twenty	30	thirty		

Money

1¢ one cent

5¢ five cents

10¢ ten cents

25¢ twenty-five cents

$1 one dollar

$5 five dollars

$10 ten dollars

$20 twenty dollars

Just the Right Word

Numbers

I have **a couple of** buttons.

a few buttons

some buttons
several buttons

a lot of buttons
many buttons

Too many buttons!

Number Order

"I am **first**."

Number Order			
1st	first	**7th**	seventh
2nd	second	**8th**	eighth
3rd	third	**9th**	ninth
4th	fourth	**10th**	tenth
5th	fifth	**11th**	eleventh
6th	sixth	**12th**	twelfth

Just the Right Word

Say Hello

When You Greet a Friend

When You Greet an Adult

Say Good-bye

When You Say Good-bye to a Friend

When You Say Good-bye to an Adult

Say Thank You

Meet New People

Ask for Help

In Your Community

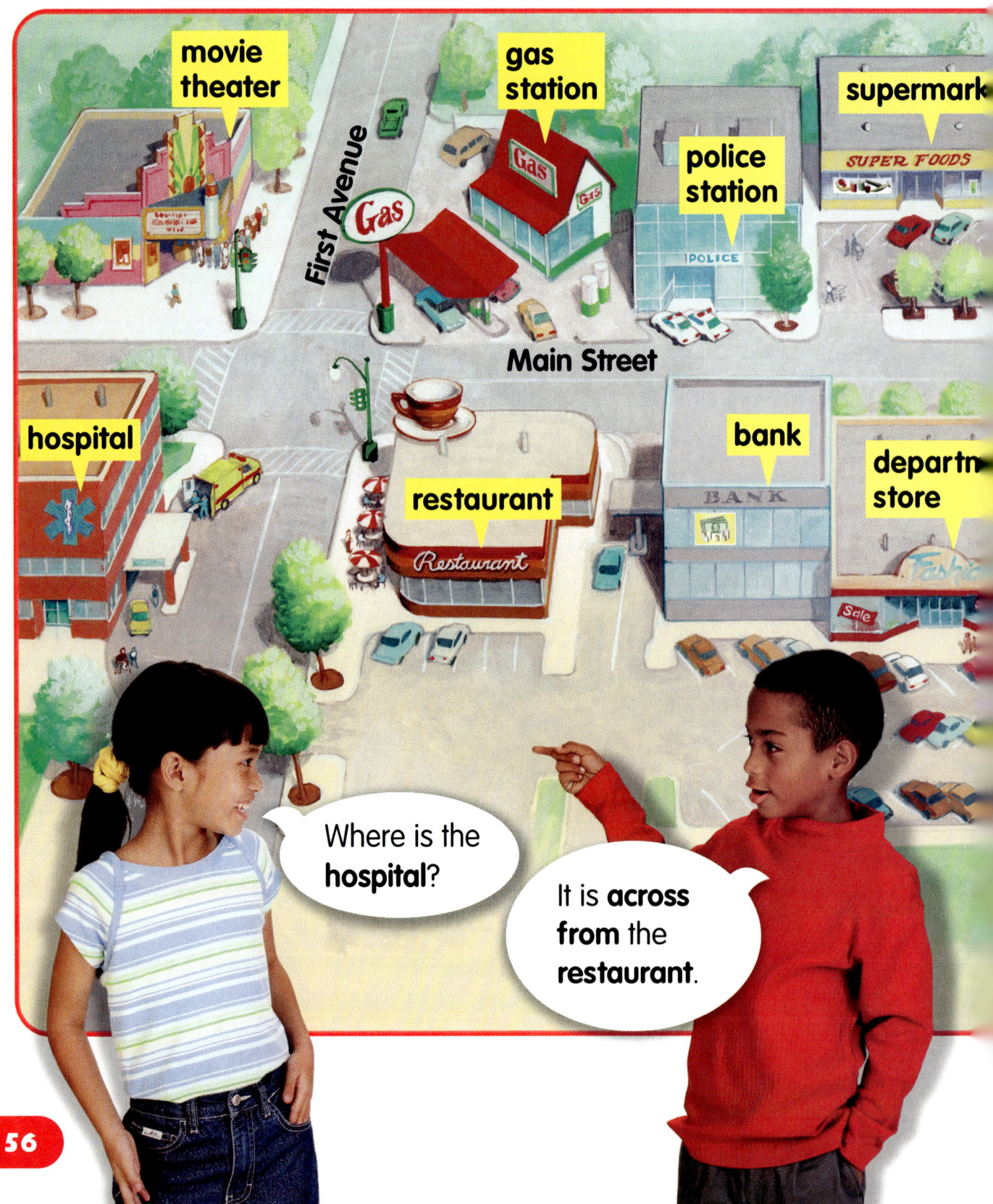

Words That Tell Where

The police station is **on** Main Street.

The gas station is **next to** the police station.

The movie theater is **across from** the gas station.

The bakery is **below** the doctor's office.

The doctor's office is **above** the bakery.

The police station is **between** the gas station and the supermarket.

Just the Right Word

Community Workers

The **farmer** works on a **farm**.

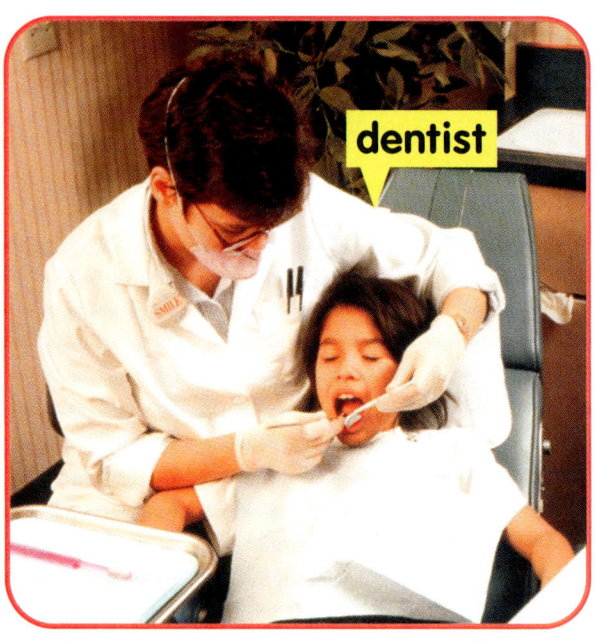

The **dentist** works in a **clinic**.

Who works in your community?

The **cashier** works in a **store**.

The **waiter** works in a **restaurant**.

The **judge** works in a **courtroom**.

The **firefighter** works in a **fire station**.

The **police officer** works all around the community.

Just the Right Word

Doctor's Office

Your Body

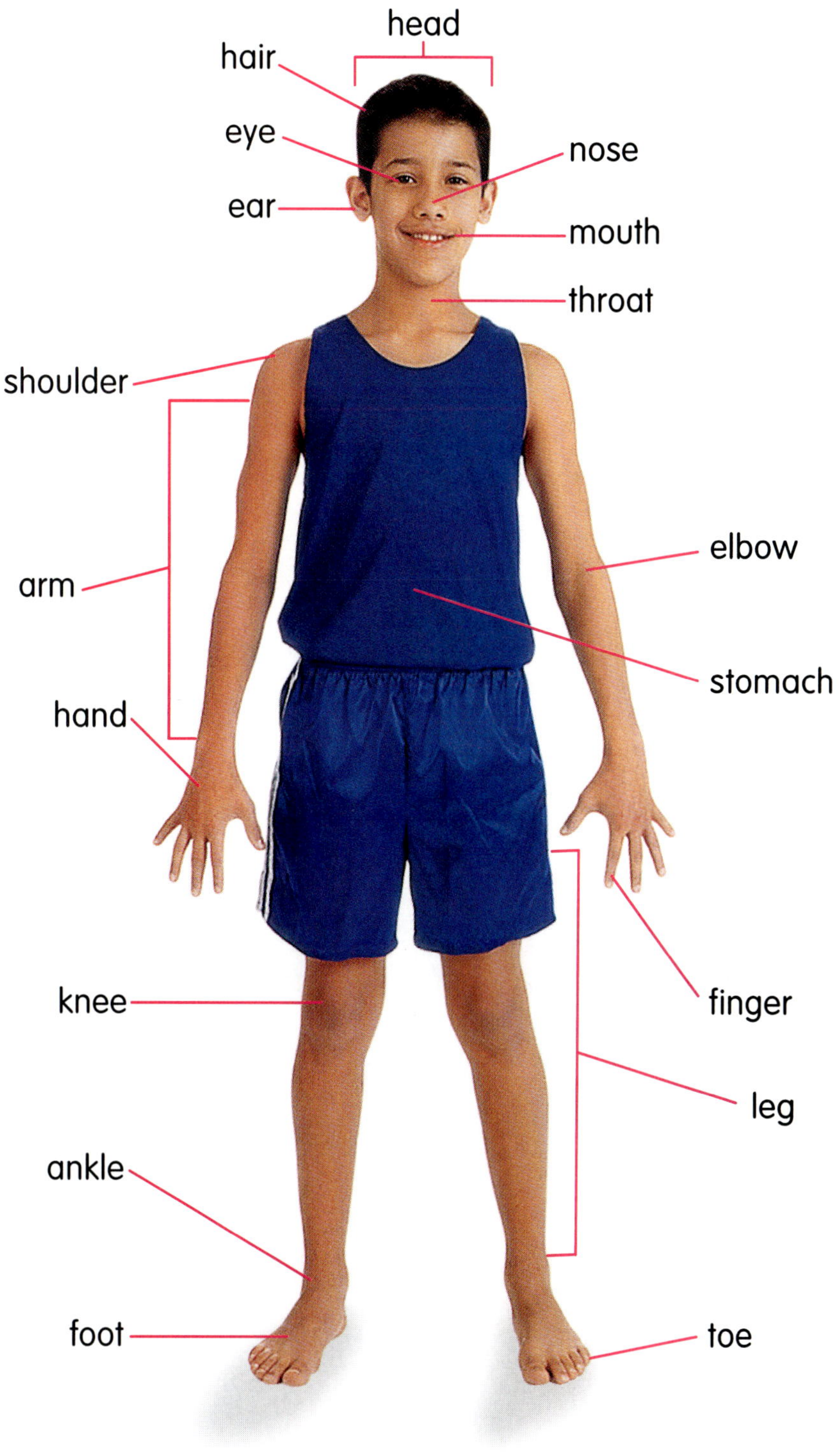

- hair
- head
- eye
- nose
- ear
- mouth
- throat
- shoulder
- arm
- elbow
- stomach
- hand
- finger
- knee
- leg
- ankle
- foot
- toe

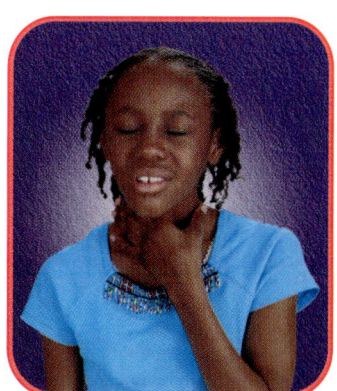

She has a **sore throat**.

He has a **stomachache**.

She has a **headache**.

Just the Right Word

Transportation

Where is the **truck** going?
It is going **down** the **street**.

taxicab

into the **tunnel**

over the **bridge**

around the **corner**

Just the Right Word

Signs and Safety

A hospital is near.

Cars have to stop here.

Slow down! Here is a school.

Cars cross the train tracks here.

People can cross the street here.

Here is the boys' bathroom.

Use this door to go outside.

Just the Right Word

Time

Days of the Week

There are seven days in a week.

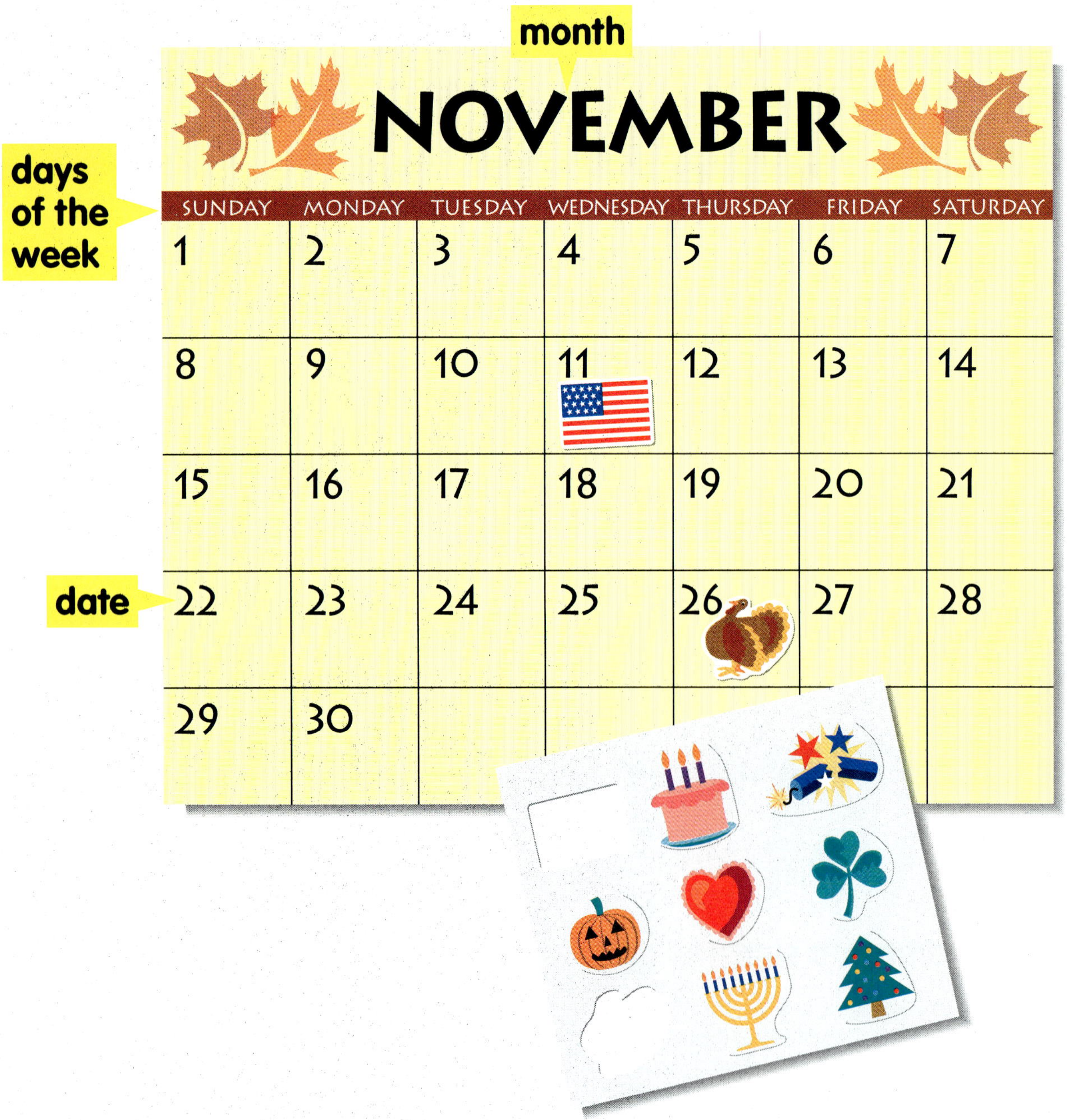

month: NOVEMBER

days of the week:

SUNDAY	MONDAY	TUESDAY	WEDNESDAY	THURSDAY	FRIDAY	SATURDAY
1	2	3	4	5	6	7
8	9	10	11	12	13	14
15	16	17	18	19	20	21
22	23	24	25	26	27	28
29	30					

date

Just the Right Word

Months

There are twelve months in a year.

January	April	July	October
February	May	August	November
March	June	September	December

Seasons

There are four seasons in a year.

spring

summer

autumn or fall

winter

Just the Right Word

Telling Time

It is **eight o'clock**.
It is time **for school**.

It is **twelve-thirty**.
It is time **for lunch**.

It is **quarter to three**.
It is time **to go home**.

It is **four forty-five**.
It is time **to do homework**.

It is **six fifteen**.
It is time **for dinner**.

It is **half-past eight**.
It is time **for bed**.

Just the Right Word

Weather

Synonyms

Synonyms are words that mean almost the same thing.

angry   **bad**

angry	bad
mad	awful
upset	terrible
bothered	horrible

big   **cold**

big	cold
large	icy
huge	chilly
enormous	freezing

go
move
walk
leave

good
great
terrific
fine

happy
glad
pleased
cheerful

like
enjoy
admire
love

little
small
tiny
wee

pretty
lovely
beautiful
cute

shout
scream
yell
holler

talk
speak
tell
say

Just the Right Word

Antonyms

Antonyms are words that have opposite meanings.

in   out

up   down

big   little

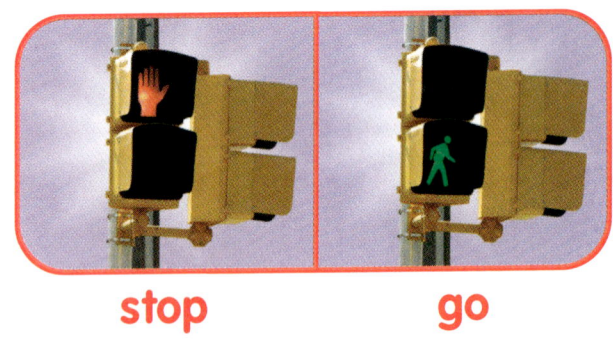

stop   go

cold   hot

good   bad

Compound Words

A **compound word** is a word made up of two smaller words.

backpack
back + pack

baseball
base + ball

bathtub
bath + tub

classroom
class + room

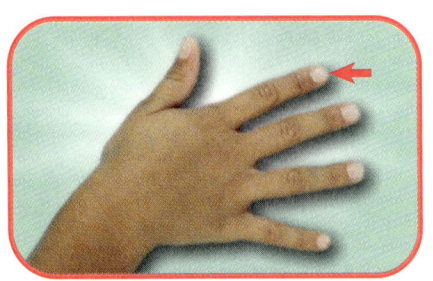
fingernail
finger + nail

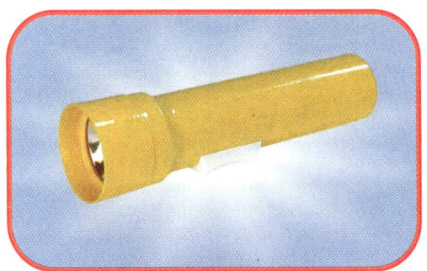
flashlight
flash + light

Just the Right Word

hairbrush
hair + brush

keyboard
key + board

mailbox
mail + box

popcorn
pop + corn

rainbow
rain + bow

sailboat
sail + boat

sidewalk
side + walk

waterfall
water + fall

Suffixes

A **suffix** is a word part that comes at the **end** of a word. A suffix changes the meaning of the word.

Suffixes	Examples
-able means "can be"	washable readable
-er means "a person who"	swimmer teacher
-ful means "full of"	helpful careful
-less means "without"	fearless colorless
-ly means "in a way that is"	quietly quickly

2+6=8

teacher

Prefixes

A **prefix** is a word part that comes at the **beginning** of a word. A prefix changes the meaning of the word.

Prefixes	Examples
dis- means "the opposite of"	disappear dislike
im-, in- mean "not"	imperfect incorrect
pre- means "before"	preview prewrite
re- means "again"	refill recycle
un- means "not"	unhappy uncomfortable

recycle

Just the Right Word

Multiple-Meaning Words

Multiple-meaning words look the same but have different meanings.

bank

The woman works at a **bank**.

The land on the side of a river is its **bank**.

bark

The dog can **bark**.

Trees have **bark**.

bat

Hit the ball with the **bat**.

A **bat** can fly.

Just the Right Word

jam

I put **jam** on my toast.

The cars are in a traffic **jam**.

leaves

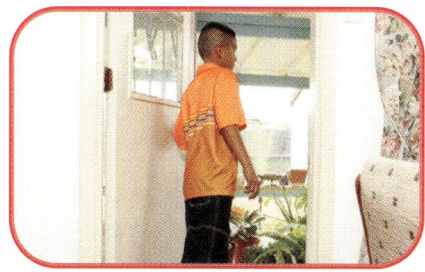
Roy **leaves** the room.

The **leaves** fall off the tree.

train

Amalia can **train** her dog.

We ride the **train**.

turn

Juji **turns** on the light.

We take **turns**.

Just the Right Word

Sound-Alike Words

Sound-alike words have the same sound when you say them, but they have different spellings and different meanings.

blue
blew

The butterfly is **blue**.

The wind **blew**.

eight
ate

A spider has **eight** legs.

I **ate** a banana.

hole
whole

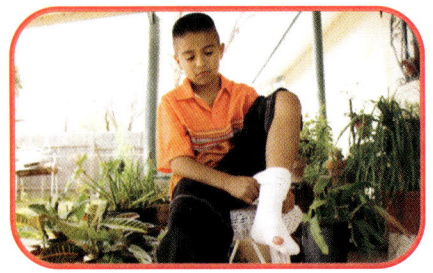

There is a **hole** in his sock.

We ate the **whole** pizza.

Just the Right Word

sail
sale

The **sail** is white.

The store has a **sale**.

son
sun

The man has a **son**.

The **sun** is hot.

won
one

They **won** the game.

I have **one** pencil.

write
right

I **write** a story.

He raises his **right** hand.

Just the Right Word

How are ideas connected? What do the parts of a story look like?

Use a picture to help you think about what you read and write.

Charts

Charts show information.
They have rows and columns.

- Go down to read a column (⬇).
- Go across to read a row (➡).

Pets in My Neighborhood

Pets		Names
cat	🐱	Fluffy
fish	🐟	Blinky
dog	🐶	Nick

column points to the Pets column. **row** points to the cat row.

Pets Owned by My Class

Pets	Total
Dogs	8
Cats	6
Hamsters	2
Birds	3
Guinea Pigs	1
Total Number of Pets	20

Picture It!

KWL Chart

A **KWL chart** helps you think about something as you study it. Read the question at the top of each column. It tells you how to complete the chart.

Topic: Pet Cats		
K What Do I **K**now?	**W** What Do I **W**ant to Learn?	**L** What Did I **L**earn?
• Cats like to eat fish. • Cats like to play. • Cats sleep a lot.	• What should cats eat and drink? • Do cats need baths?	• Cats should eat special food that is made for cats. • Cats need fresh, clean water every day. • Milk is not good for cats. • Cats keep themselves clean.

Picture It!

Clusters

A **cluster** is a picture that shows how words or ideas go together.

Web

A cluster is sometimes called a **web**.

Character Map

A cluster is sometimes called a **map**. This map tells about a story character.

Little Red Riding Hood

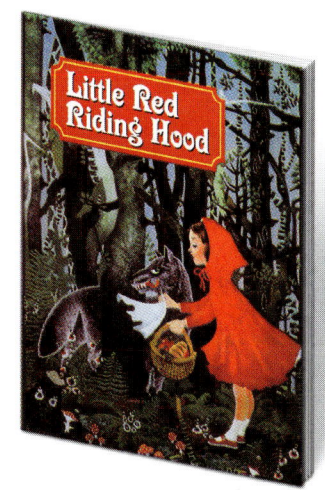

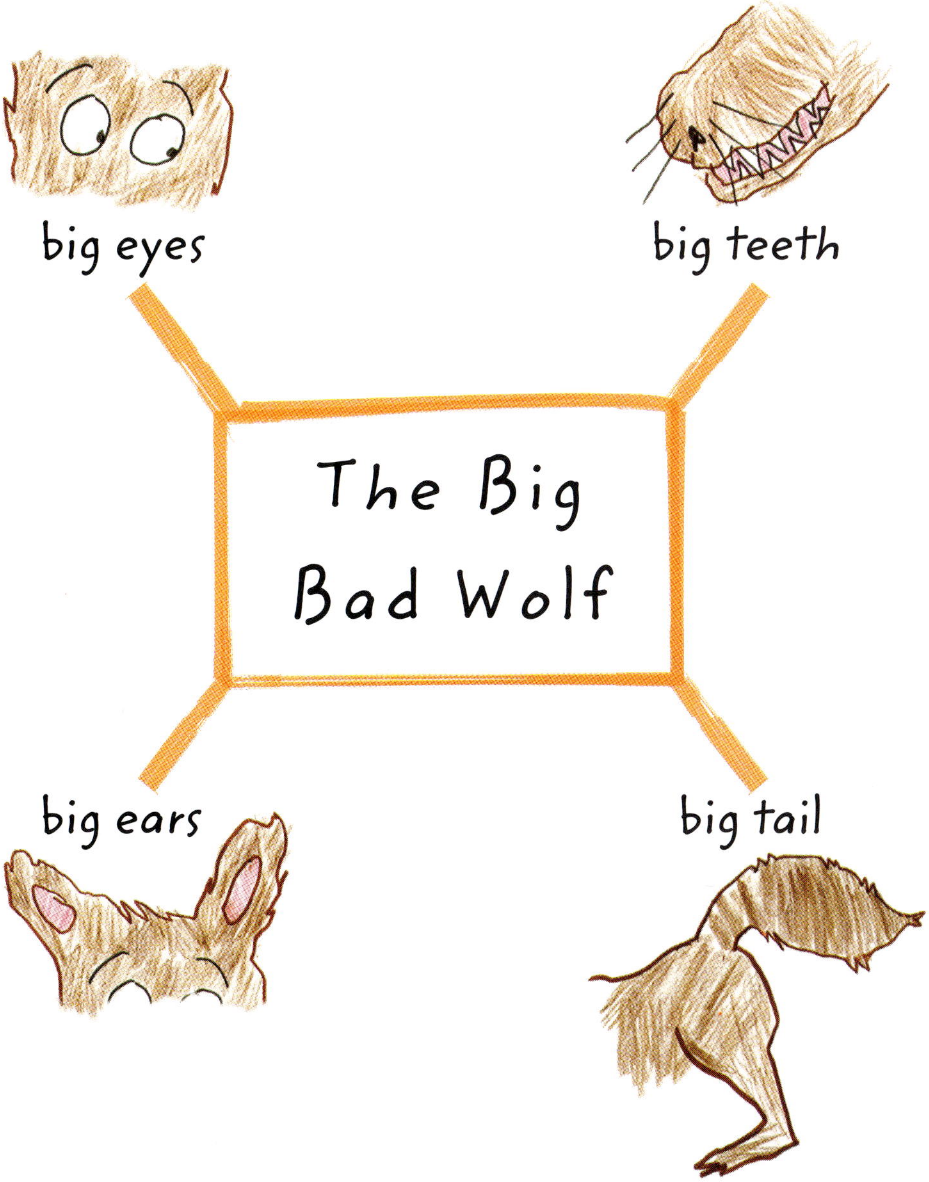

big eyes
big teeth
The Big Bad Wolf
big ears
big tail

Diagrams

A **diagram** is a picture that shows where things are, how something works, or how something happens. Words, or labels, give more information.

Parts Diagram

A **parts diagram** shows the **parts** of something. This diagram shows the parts of an oak tree.

Process Diagram

A **process diagram** shows how something changes. This diagram shows how an oak tree grows from an acorn to a full-grown tree.

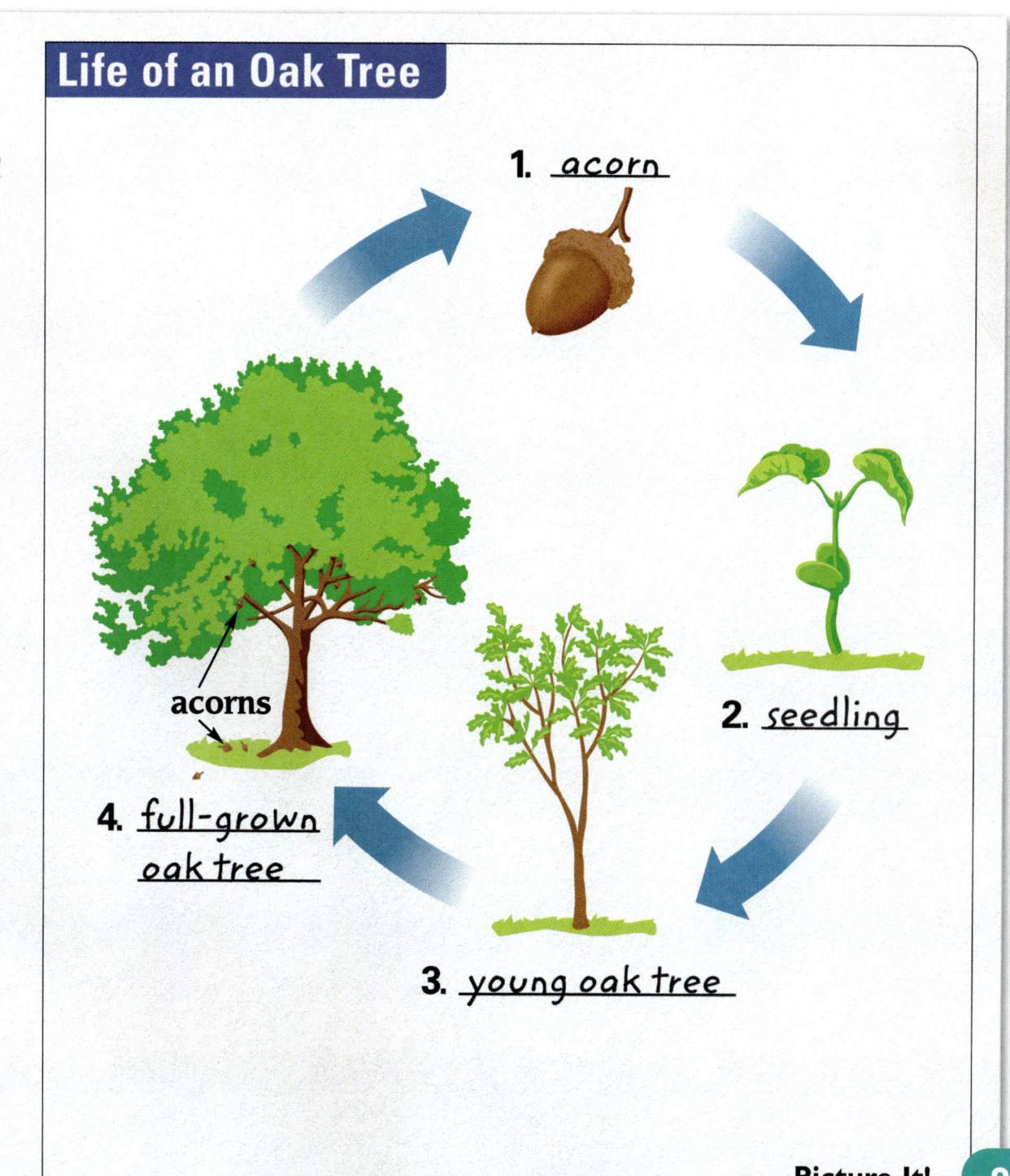

Venn Diagram

A **Venn diagram** shows how two things are the same and how they are different.

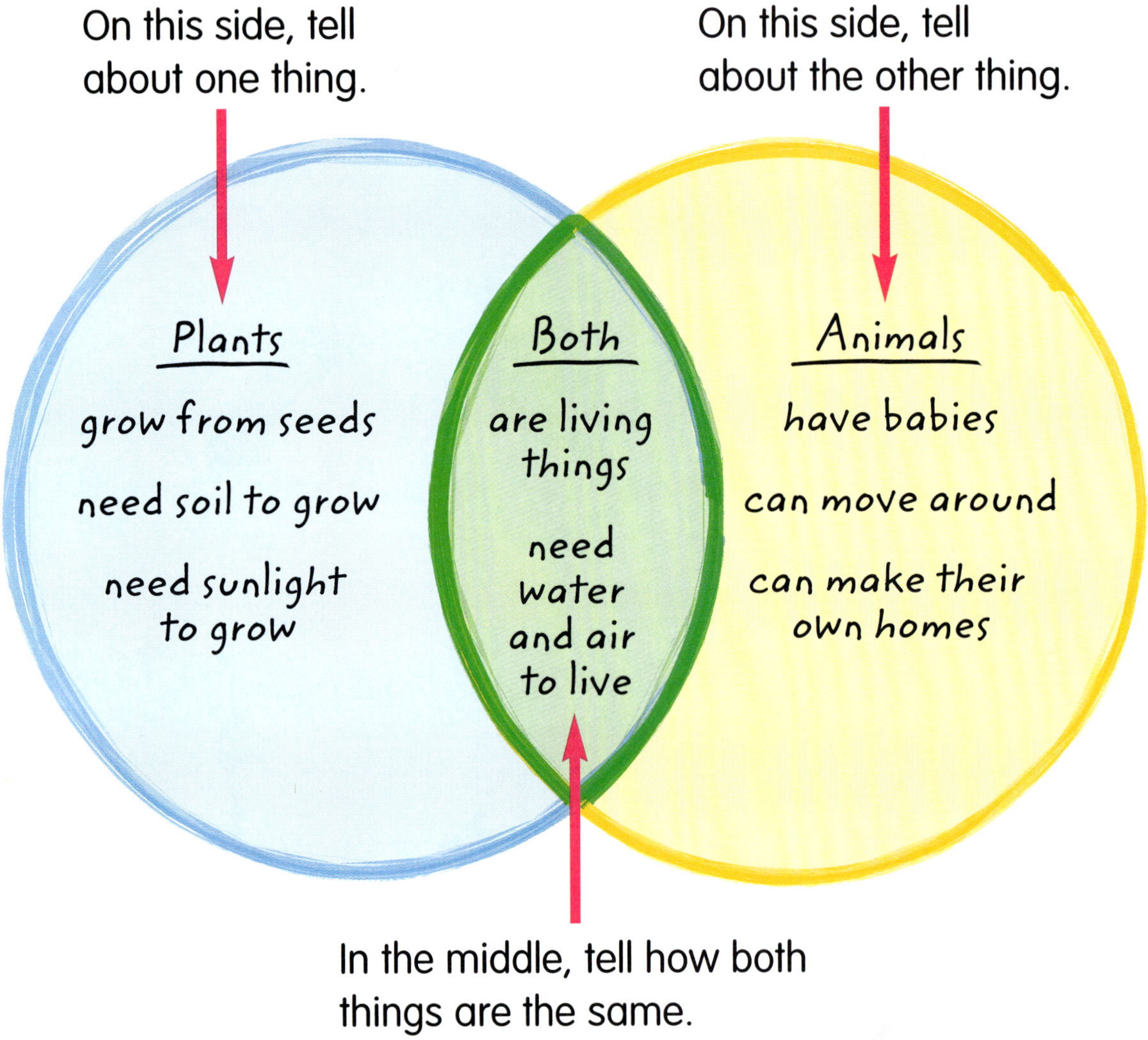

On this side, tell about one thing.

On this side, tell about the other thing.

Plants
- grow from seeds
- need soil to grow
- need sunlight to grow

Both
- are living things
- need water and air to live

Animals
- have babies
- can move around
- can make their own homes

In the middle, tell how both things are the same.

Main Idea Diagram

A **main idea diagram** shows how details are related to a main idea.

| A tree is a kind of plant. | = | A tree grows from a seed. | + | A tree needs sunlight and soil to grow. |

Main Idea — Details

| Squirrels live in trees. | + | Birds build nests in trees. | = | Trees are homes for animals. |

Details — Main Idea

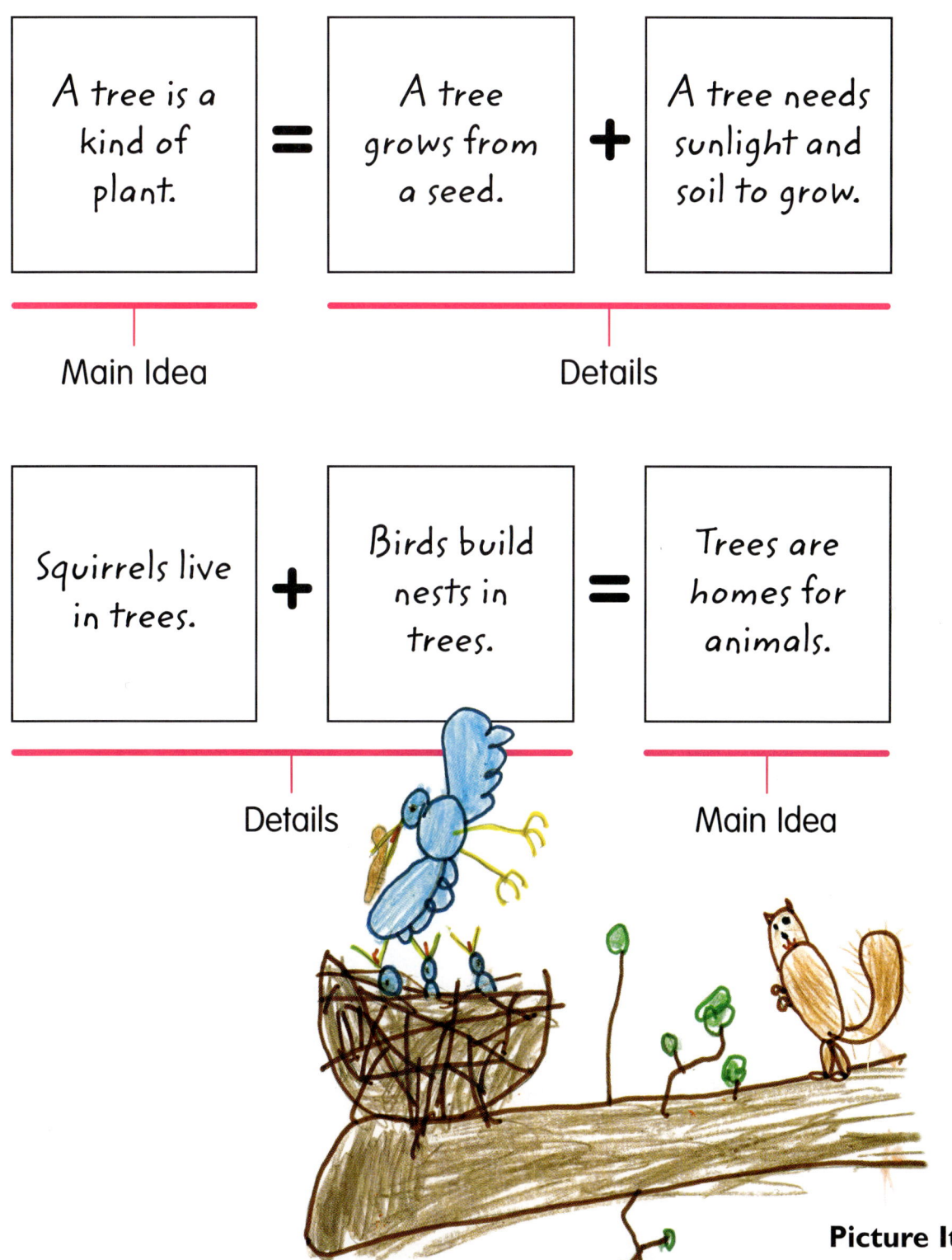

Picture It!

Graphs

A **graph** is a drawing that gives information about how many or how much there are of something.

Bar Graph

A **bar graph** uses bars to show how many or how much.

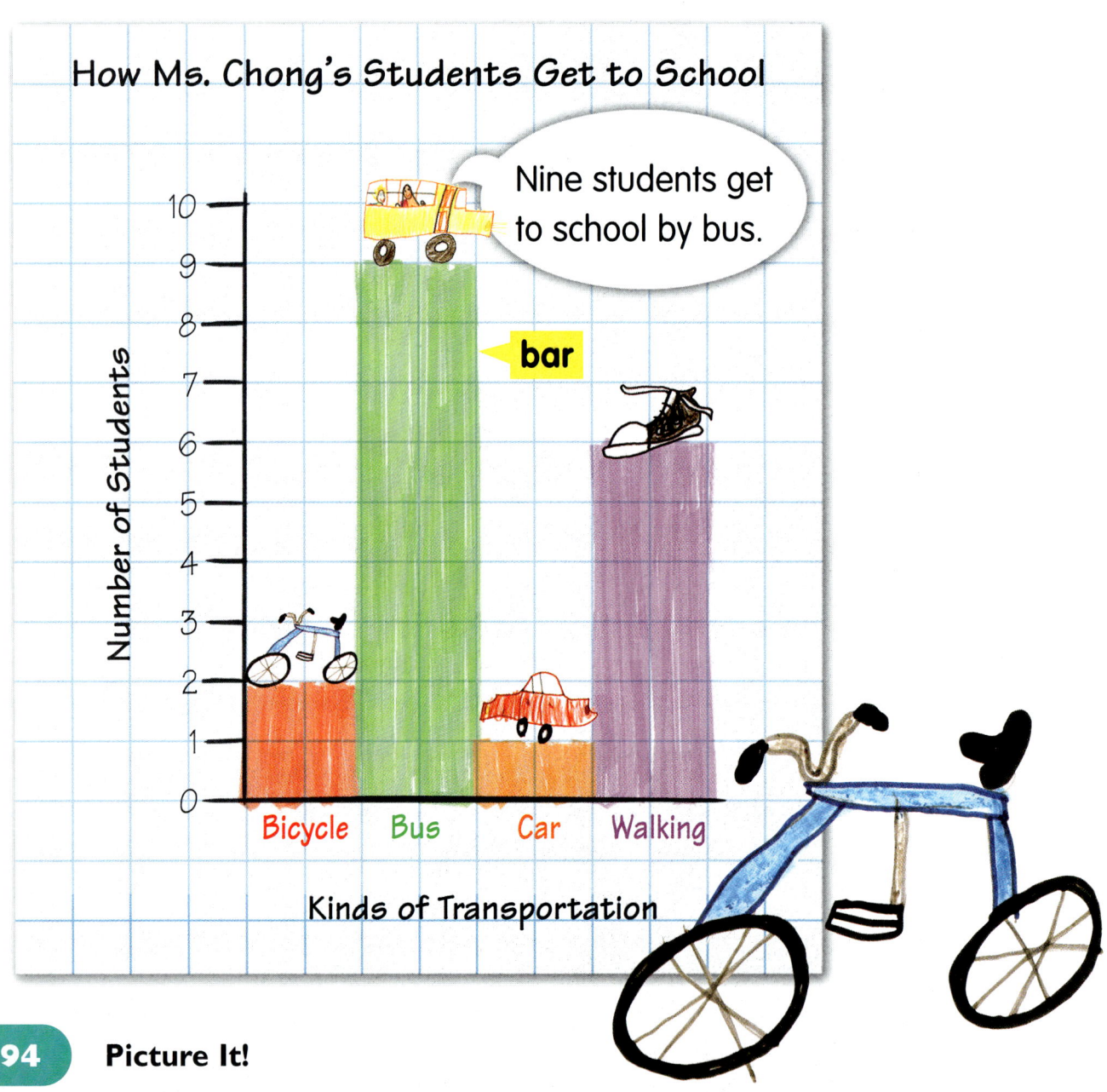

Line Graph

A **line graph** has dots. Each dot shows how many there are of something at a certain time. The dots are connected by lines.

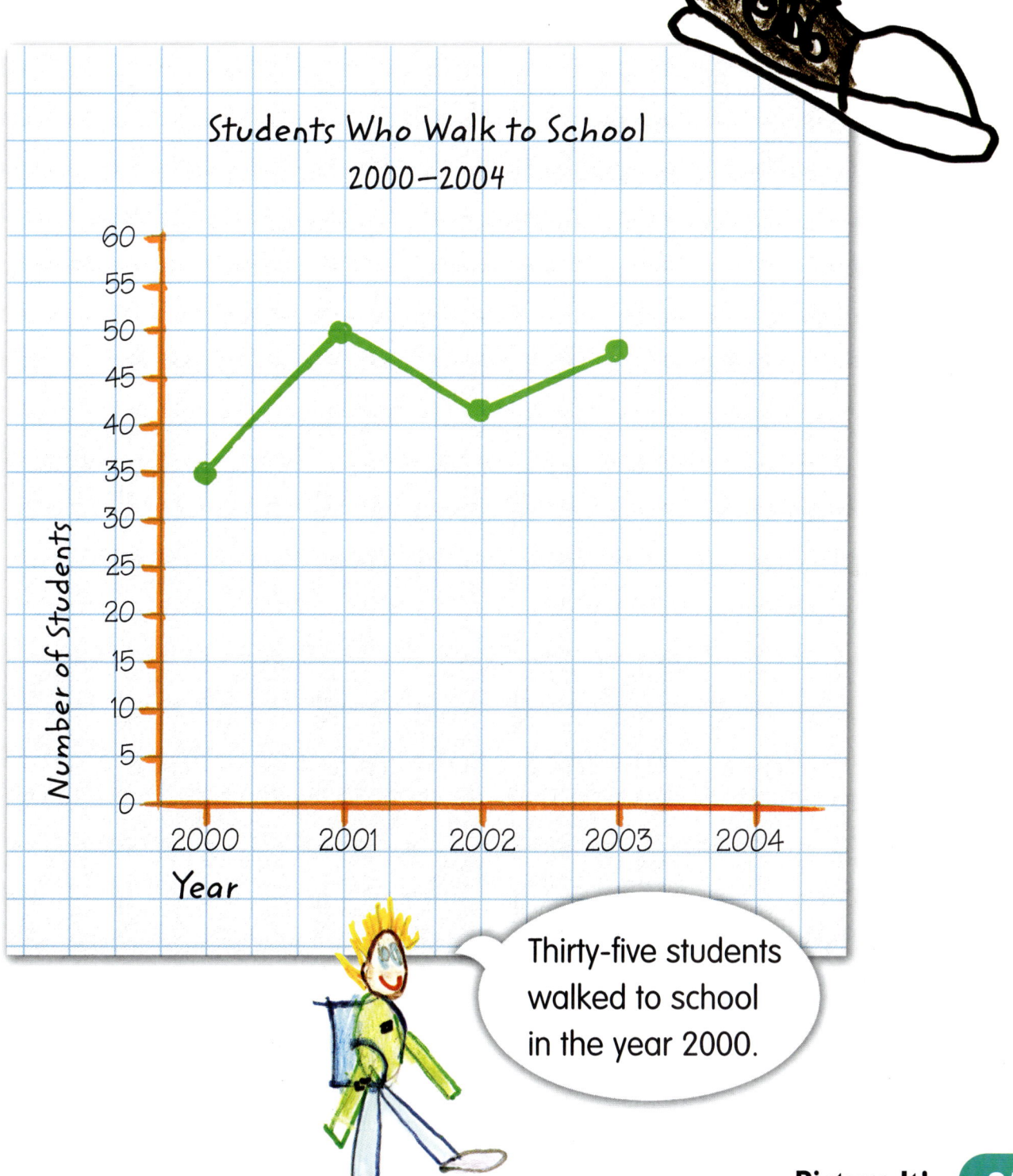

Thirty-five students walked to school in the year 2000.

Pie Graph

A **pie graph** is round like a pie. It is divided into parts. Each part is a **percentage** of the whole pie. This graph shows how many students at a school like each sport.

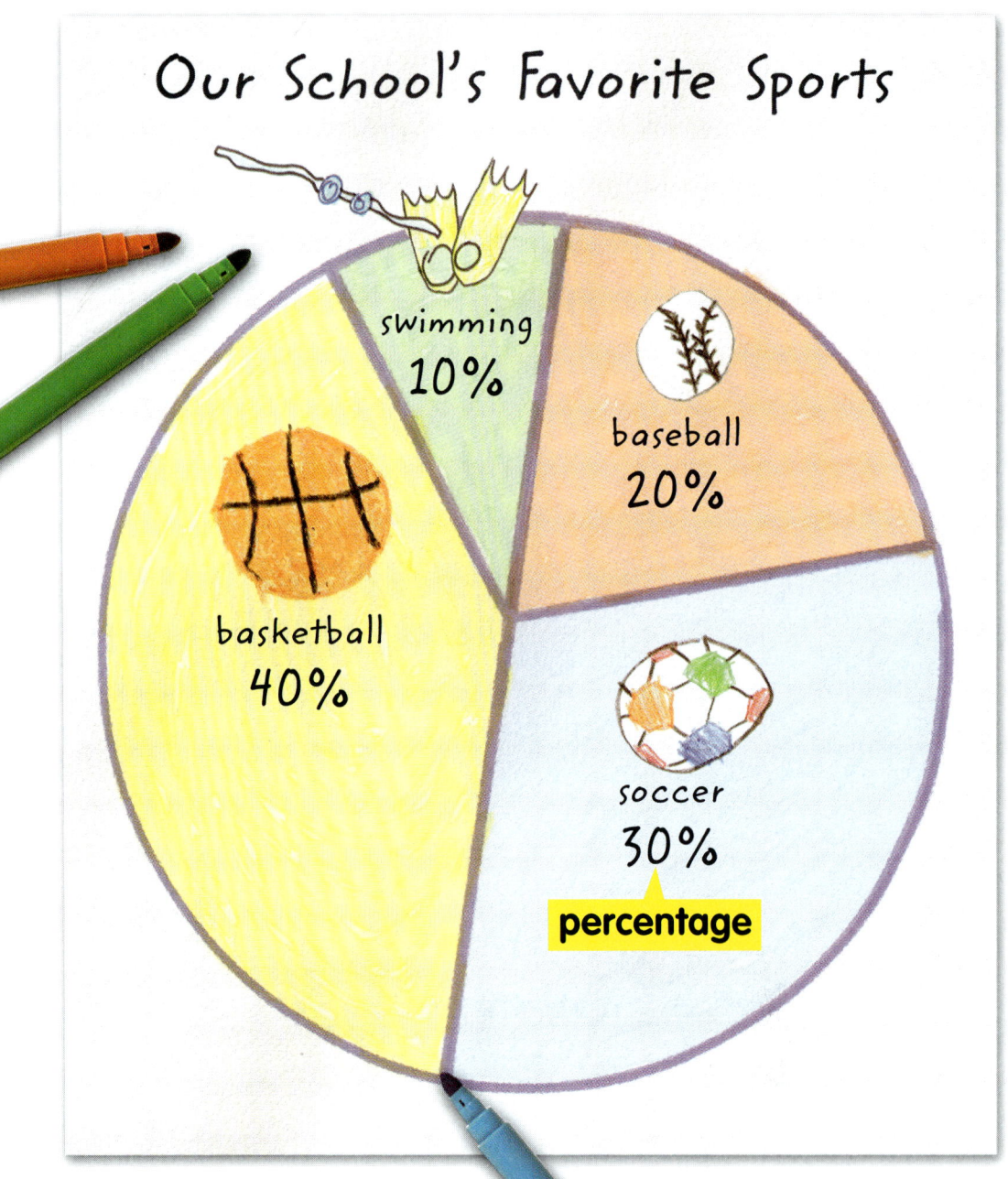

When you add up the **percentages**, they equal **100 percent**, or the whole pie.

Map

A **map** is a picture of a place. This map shows the United States. The **key** shows what each **symbol**, or picture, on the map means.

Picture It!

Story Maps

A **story map** tells about the parts of a story.

Character, Setting, and Plot

A story map can show these things:

- the **characters**, or who is in the story
- the **setting**, or where the story happens
- the **plot**, or what happens in the story.

Title: Anansi and Turtle

Character: Turtle

Setting: The woods and the river

Character: Anansi the Spider

Plot:

Turtle visits Anansi in the woods.
Anansi does not want to share his dinner with Turtle.
So he plays a trick on Turtle.
The trick helps Anansi keep his dinner.

Months later, Anansi visits Turtle in the river.
This time, Turtle plays a trick on Anansi.
The trick helps Turtle keep his own dinner.

Beginning, Middle, and End

This story map tells what happens in each part of the story.

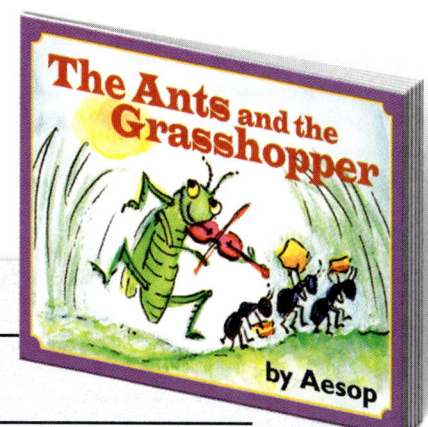

Title: The Ants and the Grasshopper

Author: Aesop

Beginning
The ants gather food all summer. They store it for the winter. The grasshopper sings and plays.

Middle
The ants warn the grasshopper to save food for himself. But the grasshopper does not want to work. When winter comes, the grasshopper is cold and hungry.

End
The ants feel sorry for the grasshopper. They share their food with him. Then the grasshopper plays music for the ants.

Picture It!

Sequence Chain

This story map shows the order, or **sequence**, in which story events happen.

Title: The Fox and the Crow

Author: Aesop

First: Crow sits in a tree. She has a piece of cheese in her beak. Fox sees the cheese and wants it.

Next: Fox tells Crow that she is beautiful. He says she must have a beautiful voice, too. Fox asks Crow to sing.

Then: Crow opens her beak to sing and drops the cheese.

Last: Fox catches the cheese and eats it!

Problem-and-Solution Map

Some stories are all about a **problem** and how the problem gets solved, or its **solution**.

Title: It Could Always Be Worse

Characters: a farmer, his wife and children, and a wise man
Setting: a one-room house

Problem: A farmer lives in a one-room house with his wife and six children. It is too crowded.

Event 1: The farmer asks a wise man for help. The wise man tells the farmer to bring the pigs and the chickens into the house.

Event 2: Now the house is very crowded. The wise man tells the farmer to bring the other animals into the house.

Event 3: Now the house is full! There is no more room. The wise man tells the farmer to take all the animals out of the house.

Solution: The farmer thinks the house is not crowded anymore.

Goal-and-Outcome Map

In some stories, a character tries to reach a **goal**. The goal is what the character tries to get or do, or where the character wants to go. The **outcome** is what happens at the end.

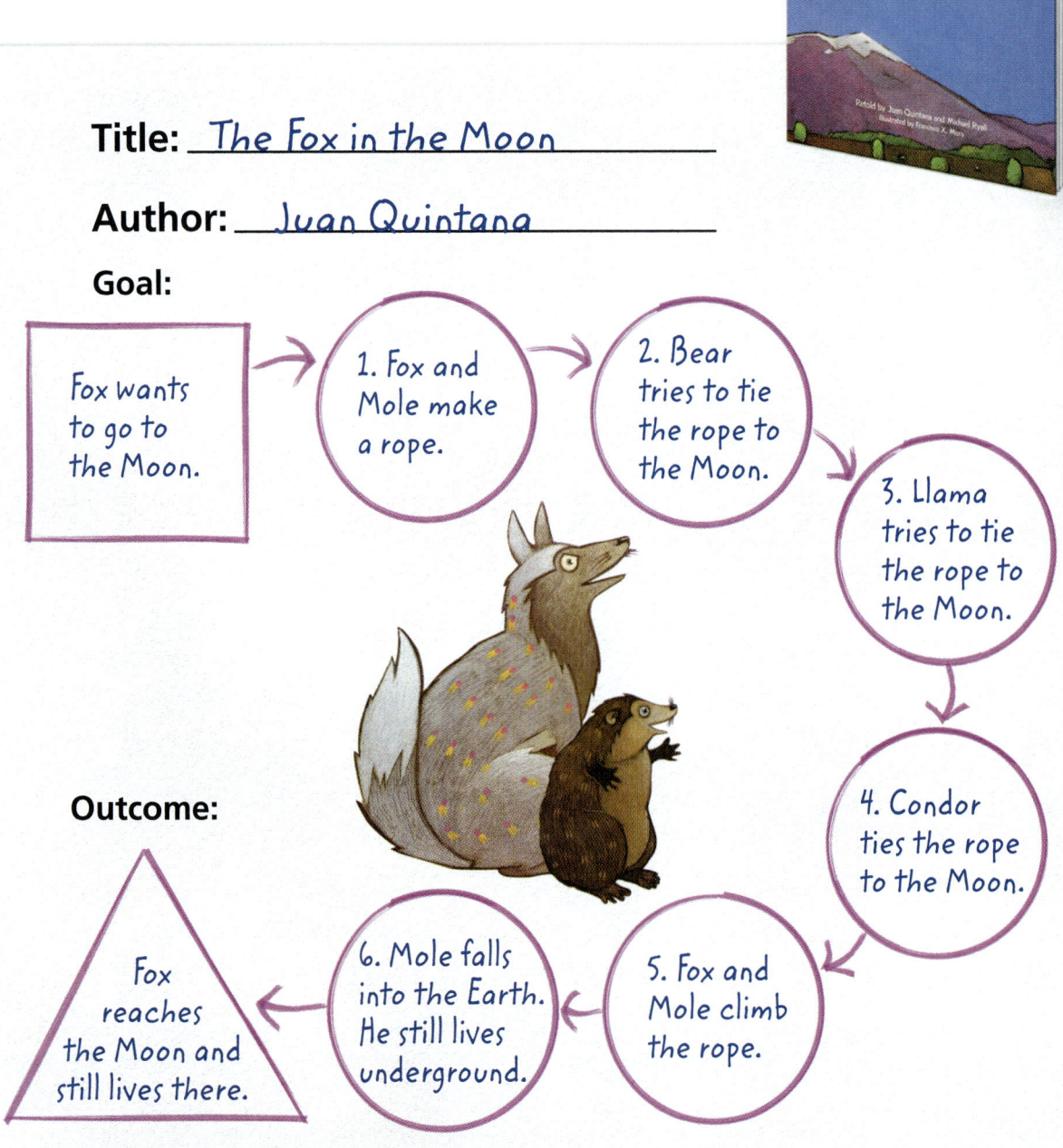

Title: _The Fox in the Moon_

Author: _Juan Quintana_

Goal: Fox wants to go to the Moon.

1. Fox and Mole make a rope.
2. Bear tries to tie the rope to the Moon.
3. Llama tries to tie the rope to the Moon.
4. Condor ties the rope to the Moon.
5. Fox and Mole climb the rope.
6. Mole falls into the Earth. He still lives underground.

Outcome: Fox reaches the Moon and still lives there.

Picture It!

Cause-and-Effect Map

A **cause-and-effect map** shows the events in a story and why they happen.

Title: Two of Everything

Author: Lily Toy Hong

Cause	Effect
Mr. Haktak finds a brass pot. He puts his purse with five gold coins into the pot.	He finds two purses with five gold coins each inside the pot.
Mrs. Haktak's hairpin falls into the pot.	She finds two hairpins in the pot.
Mr. Haktak puts his winter coat into the pot.	He finds two winter coats in the pot.
The Haktaks put coins into the pot.	The pot is filled with coins.
Mrs. Haktak falls into the pot. Mr. Haktak falls into the pot.	Now there are two Mrs. Haktaks and two Mr. Haktaks.

Picture It! 103

Time Lines

A **time line** lists when important events happen. It tells about each event in the order that it happened. This time line shows special events in a person's life. Read it from left to right (➔).

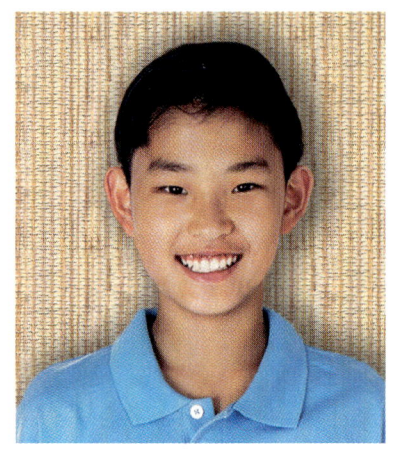

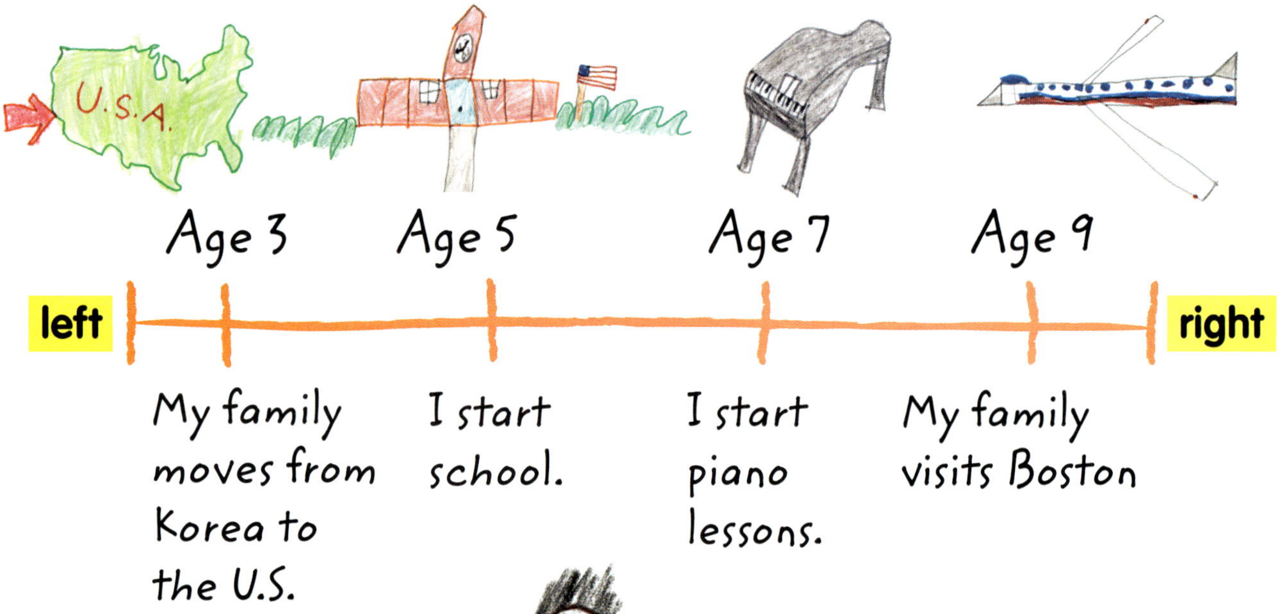

U.S.A.
Age 3
Age 5
Age 7
Age 9
left
right
My family moves from Korea to the U.S.
I start school.
I start piano lessons.
My family visits Boston

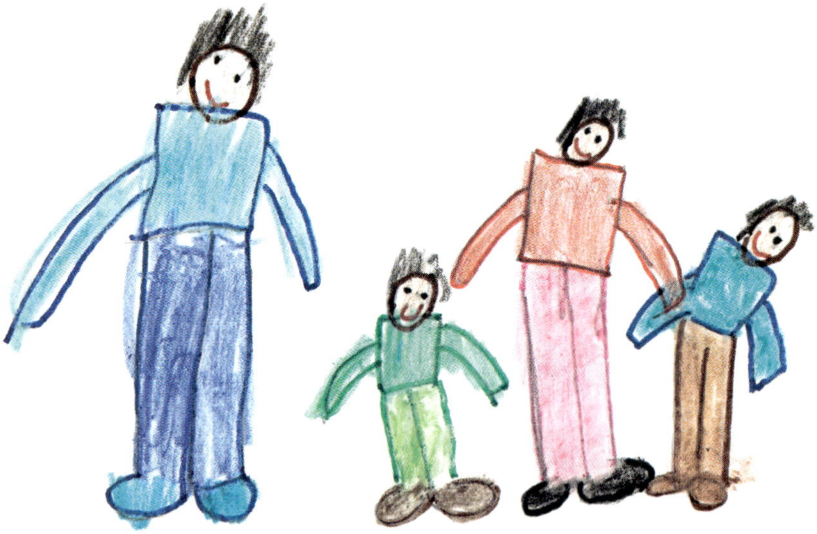

This time line tells about inventions.
Read it from top to bottom (⬇).

top

Inventions

 **1876**
Alexander Graham Bell invents the telephone.

1879
Thomas Edison invents the electric lightbulb.

 **1908**
Henry Ford invents the Model T car.

1923
Garrett A. Morgan invents the traffic light.

 **1927**
Philo Farnsworth invents the television.

1945
The first electronic computer is invented.

bottom

Picture It! 105

Chapter 3
Put It in Writing!

What do you want to tell people? How do you want to say it?

Just follow the steps to put your ideas in writing.

The Writing Process

The **Writing Process** has five steps. Follow these steps to make your writing better.

STEP 1 Prewrite

Plan what you will write.

- **Think of ideas.** Make a list or draw pictures. Collect your ideas in a writing file.

- **Choose an idea.** Look at your writing file. Which idea do you like best? Choose one. This will be your **topic**.

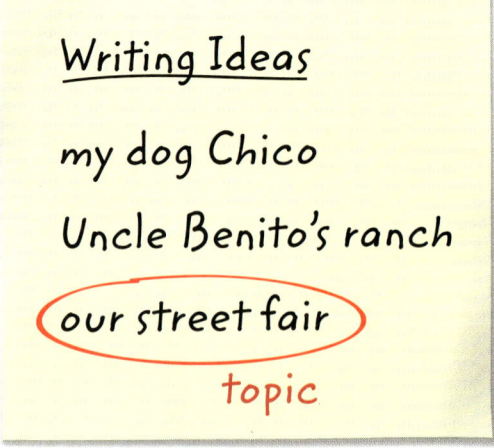

Writing Process

■ **Choose your purpose, audience, and form.**
Ask yourself these questions. They will help you decide how to write about your topic.

1. Why are you writing? This is your **purpose**.

2. Who is going to read your writing? This is your **audience**.

3. What are you writing? This is your **form**.

You can make an **FATP** chart to help you remember.

Form:	A description
Audience:	My classmates
Topic:	The street fair
Purpose:	To describe something

I will write a description to tell my class about the street fair.

Prewrite, continued

■ **Think about what you know.** What do you already know about your topic? Collect details. Here are two ways.

- You can make a **cluster**.

- You can make a **5Ws chart**.

TOPIC: Our Street Fair	
Who?	neighbors, Mrs. Vega, Mr. Guerra
What?	games, food, music, dancing, stories
When?	last week
Where?	my street
Why?	fun!

Put It in Writing!

■ **Organize your details.** A **diagram** is one way to organize details. It can help you decide what order to use when you write.

Topic: Our Street Fair
1. music, danced
2. piñata
3. Mrs. Vega's tamales
4. Mr. Guerra told stories

Write your topic here.

List your details in order.

Mr. Guerra told stories after we ate. I will put that detail last.

STEP 2 Draft

When you write your **first draft**, you turn ideas into sentences. You use the sentences to make paragraphs. Write your draft quickly. You can correct mistakes later.

■ Write a **topic sentence** to tell the main idea of a paragraph.

■ Write more sentences to add the **details**.

Put It in Writing!

Keys to the Computer

Writing Process

You can use the computer to **write your draft**.

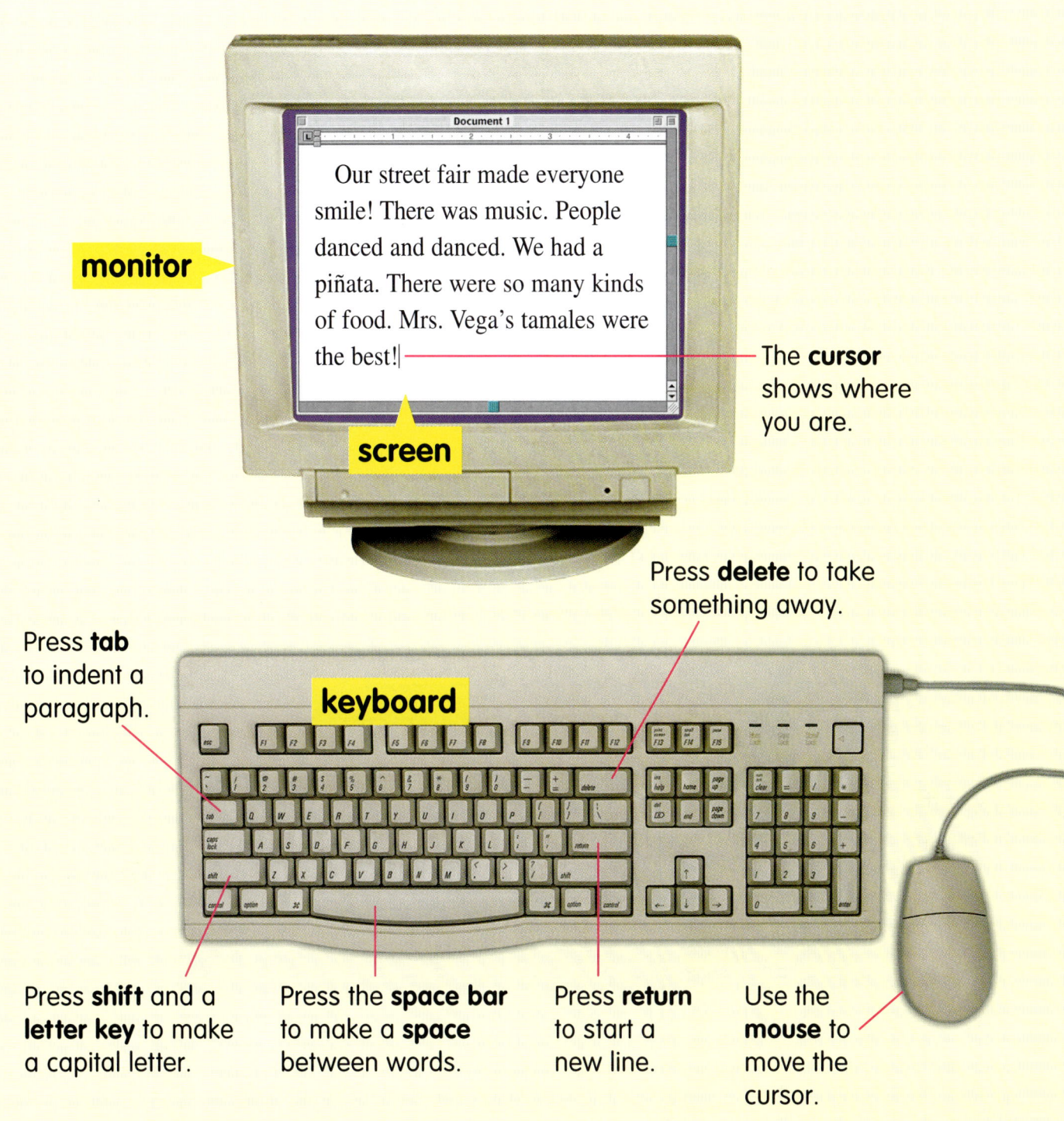

- **monitor**
- **screen**
- The **cursor** shows where you are.
- Press **delete** to take something away.
- Press **tab** to indent a paragraph.
- **keyboard**
- Press **shift** and a **letter key** to make a capital letter.
- Press the **space bar** to make a **space** between words.
- Press **return** to start a new line.
- Use the **mouse** to move the cursor.

Put It in Writing!

STEP
3 Revise

When you **revise**, you make changes. They make your writing better and clearer.

■ Read your draft. Ask yourself these questions:

✓ Did I say what I wanted to say?
✓ Are the sentences in the right order?
✓ Will my readers understand?
✓ Is my writing interesting?

Maybe I should say exactly how the tamales tasted.

Our street fair made everyone smile! There was music. People danced and danced. We had a piñata. There were so many kinds of food. Mrs. Vega's tamales were the best!

The kids also got to play a lot of games. And then we listened to Mr. Guerra's stories.

Is this detail about the piñata in the right place?

I need to say more about Mr. Guerra's stories.

Put It in Writing!

Writing Process

■ Have a partner read your draft two times. Discuss your draft in a **peer conference**.

The reader should:	The writer should:
Say what the writing is about. Tell what you like best. *"This is about a street fair. I like the part about tamales."*	Listen carefully.
Ask questions. Tell how to make the writing better. *"Can you add more details about the music?"*	Think about your partner's ideas. *"Good idea! I'll tell more about the salsa band."*

Put It in Writing!

Revising, continued

■ Make your changes. Use the **revising marks**.

Revising Marks

Mark	Meaning
∧	Add.
⌒	Take out.
∧	Change to this.
⟲	Move to here.

These details give a clearer picture.

This sentence is out of order. It belongs with games.

Our street fair made everyone smile!
There was music. People danced and danced.
  A band played salsa   All the neighbors
We had a piñata. There were so many kinds
of food. Mrs. Vega's tamales were the best!
                    spicy
The kids also got to play a lot of games.
And then we listened to Mr. Guerra's stories.

Now my readers will know how the tamales tasted.

STEP

4 Edit and Proofread

When you **edit and proofread**, you look for mistakes. When you find a mistake, fix it. Follow these steps:

1. Read your writing.
2. Make sure words are spelled correctly.
3. Look for mistakes in capitalization, grammar, and punctuation.
4. Use **proofreading marks** to show what you need to fix.

Proofreading Marks

Mark	Meaning
^	Add.
^,	Add a comma.
⊙	Add a period.
≡	Capitalize.
◯	Check spelling.
/	Make lowercase.
⌒	Take out.

The kids also got to play a lot of games. We had a piñata. ~~And~~ then we listened to Mr. Guerra's stories. They were funny. He made his voice sound like different Animals⊙ His bear voice really made us laff.

Keys to the Computer

If you write on the computer, you can also use it to **check your spelling**. Follow these steps to check the spelling of all the words in your writing:

STEP 1 Click on **Tools** in the toolbar. You will see a menu.

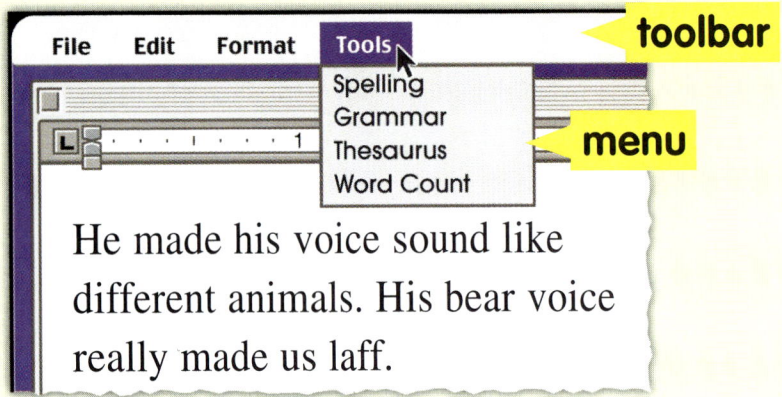

STEP 2 Click on **Spelling** in the menu. The computer will show misspelled words in color.

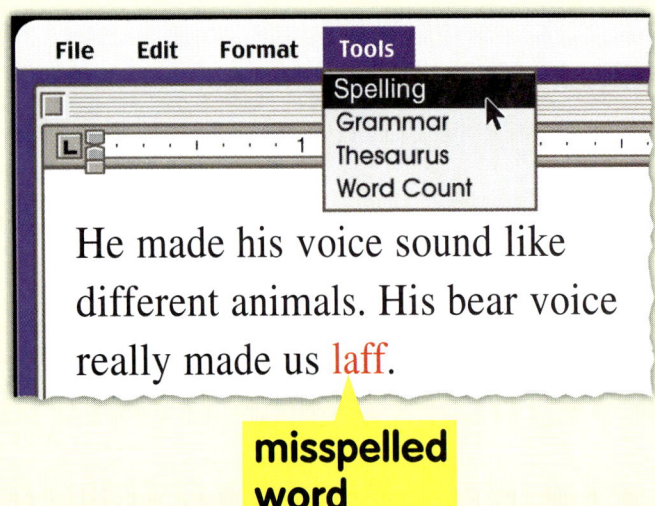

Writing Process

STEP 3 The computer will show you a list of **suggestions**. Click on the word you want.

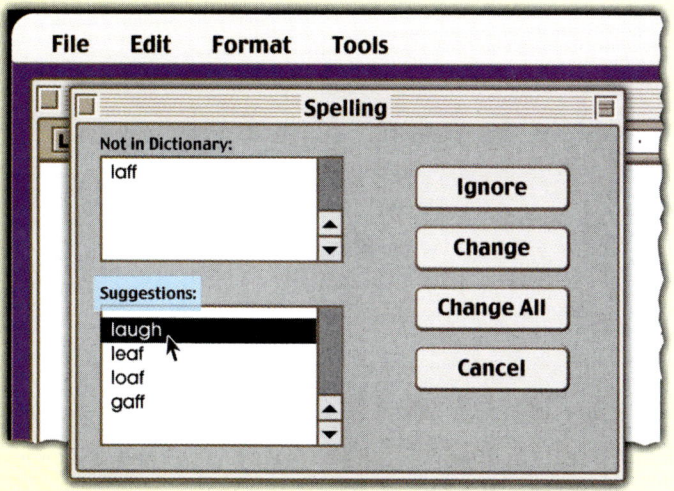

STEP 4 Click on the **Change** button. This corrects the spelling of the word in your writing.

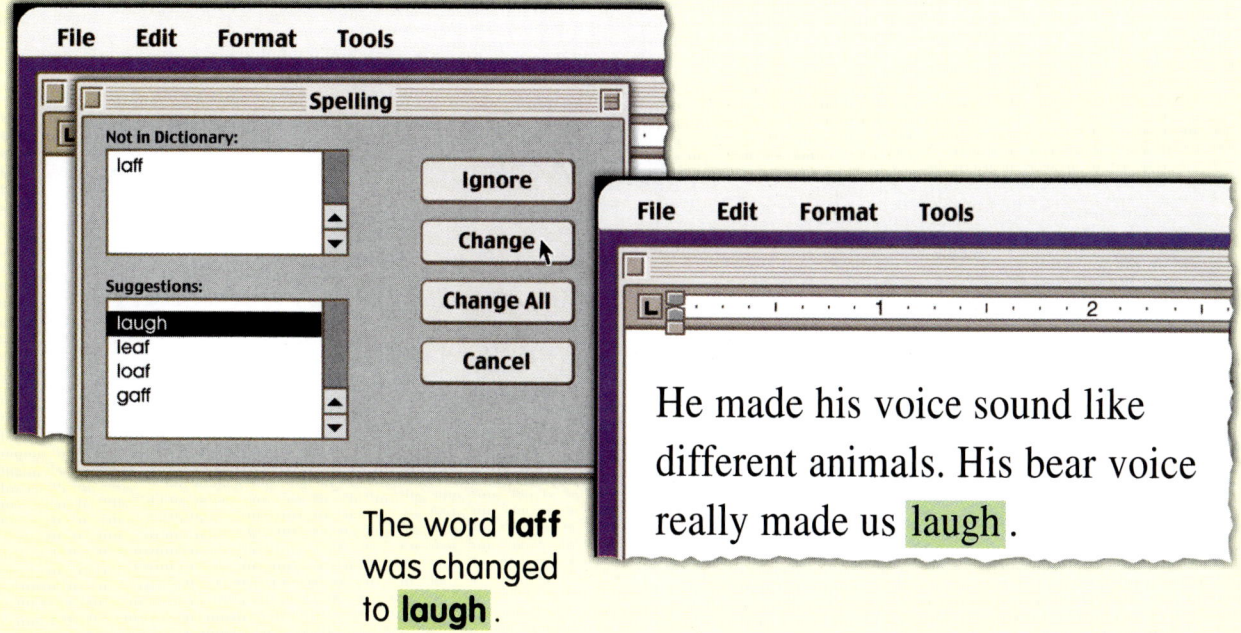

The word **laff** was changed to **laugh**.

He made his voice sound like different animals. His bear voice really made us **laugh**.

Put It in Writing! 119

STEP
5 Publish

To **publish** means to present, or show, your work. You make a final copy of your writing. Then you share it. You can:

- Read your work out loud to a classmate.
- E-mail your work to a family member or friend.
- Turn your work into a book.
- Turn your work into a play. Act it out.

Our Street Fair
by Angela Alonso

Our street fair made everyone smile! A band played salsa music. All the neighbors danced and danced. There were many kinds of food. Mrs. Vega's spicy tamales were the best!

The kids also got to play a lot of games. We had a piñata. Then we listened to Mr. Guerra's stories. They were funny. He made his voice sound like different animals. His bear voice really made us laugh.

Keys to the Computer

Writing Process

You can use the computer and a **printer** to **publish your writing**. Follow these steps:

1. Turn on the printer. Make sure there is paper in the **paper tray**.

2. Click on **File** in the computer toolbar. Click on **Print** in the menu.

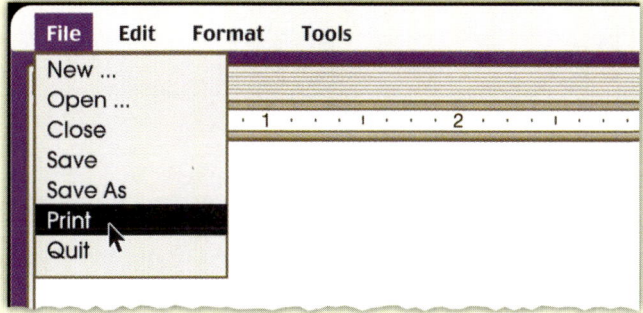

3. How many **copies** do you want? Type a number in the box. Click on **Print** to start printing.

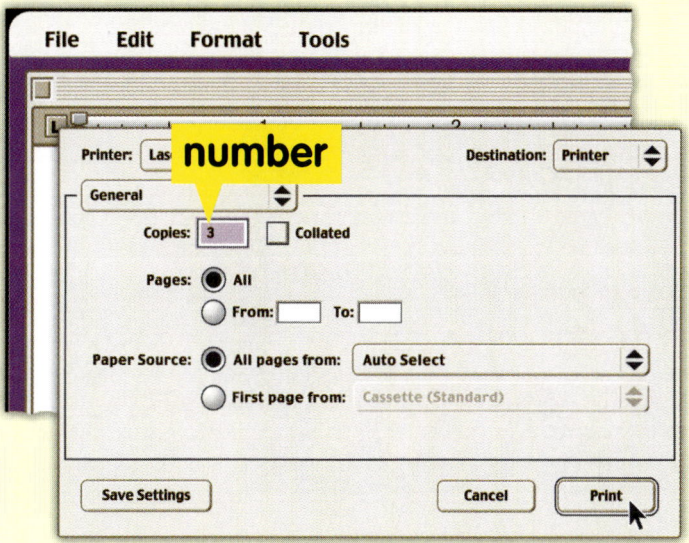

Put It in Writing! 121

Kinds of Writing

Announcement

An **announcement** is a short message. It tells about a special event, such as a play, festival, or other fun activity.

Tell what the event is.

Tell **when** and **where** the event will be.

Give details.

Put It in Writing!

Book Review

Do you want to tell about a book you read? Then write a **book review**.

Tell the **title** of the book. Underline the title.

Name the **author**.

My Review of Dear Juno

Dear Juno is a book by Soyung Pak. It tells about a boy named Juno who lives in the United States. Juno writes letters to his grandmother.

She lives in Korea. Grandmother writes back in Korean, but Juno cannot read it! Then Grandmother sends photos. They help Juno understand.

I like this book because it tells about ways that people can share the important things in their lives. The book has beautiful pictures, too!

Tell what the book is about.

Did you like the book? Tell why or why not.

Put It in Writing!

Description

A **description** tells what someone or something is like.

Description of a Person

You can describe a real or made-up person. Use words that help your reader "see" the person.

My Best Friend

My best friend is Theo. He has dark hair and brown eyes. He is smaller than me, but he can run faster!

Theo likes to build things. He likes to help people learn things, too. Theo showed me how to build a model airplane. Now we are building a clubhouse together.

- Name the person.
- Tell what the person looks like. Use **describing words**.
- Tell about the person's **actions**.
- What is special or interesting about the person? Give **details** and **examples**.

Description of a Place

You can describe a real or made-up place. Use details to help your readers "see" the place.

Name the place in the **topic sentence**.

Use **sensory words** to tell how things look, sound, feel, smell, or taste.

Use **location words** to tell where things are.

My Uncle's Garden

My uncle's garden looks like a rainbow. Uncle Luis grows all kinds of vegetables and fruits there. He has **smooth**, **green** watermelons and **bright yellow** peppers. He grows **red**, **juicy** tomatoes. There are **small**, **pink** flowers **all around** the garden. That's why his garden smells so **sweet**.

My uncle's garden is **noisy**, too. Bees buzz **in and out** of the flowers. Birds chirp and sing **above** my head. I love to listen to my uncle's garden!

Put It in Writing! 125

Directions

Some **directions** tell how to make something. Others tell how to get to a place. Always put the steps in your directions in order.

How to Make Something

The list of **materials** tells you what to use.

The **steps** have numbers to show the order.

How to Get to a Place

Use **direction words**. They tell people which way to go.

Add **details** to describe the place so that people can find it.

Draw a map. It helps people see where to go.

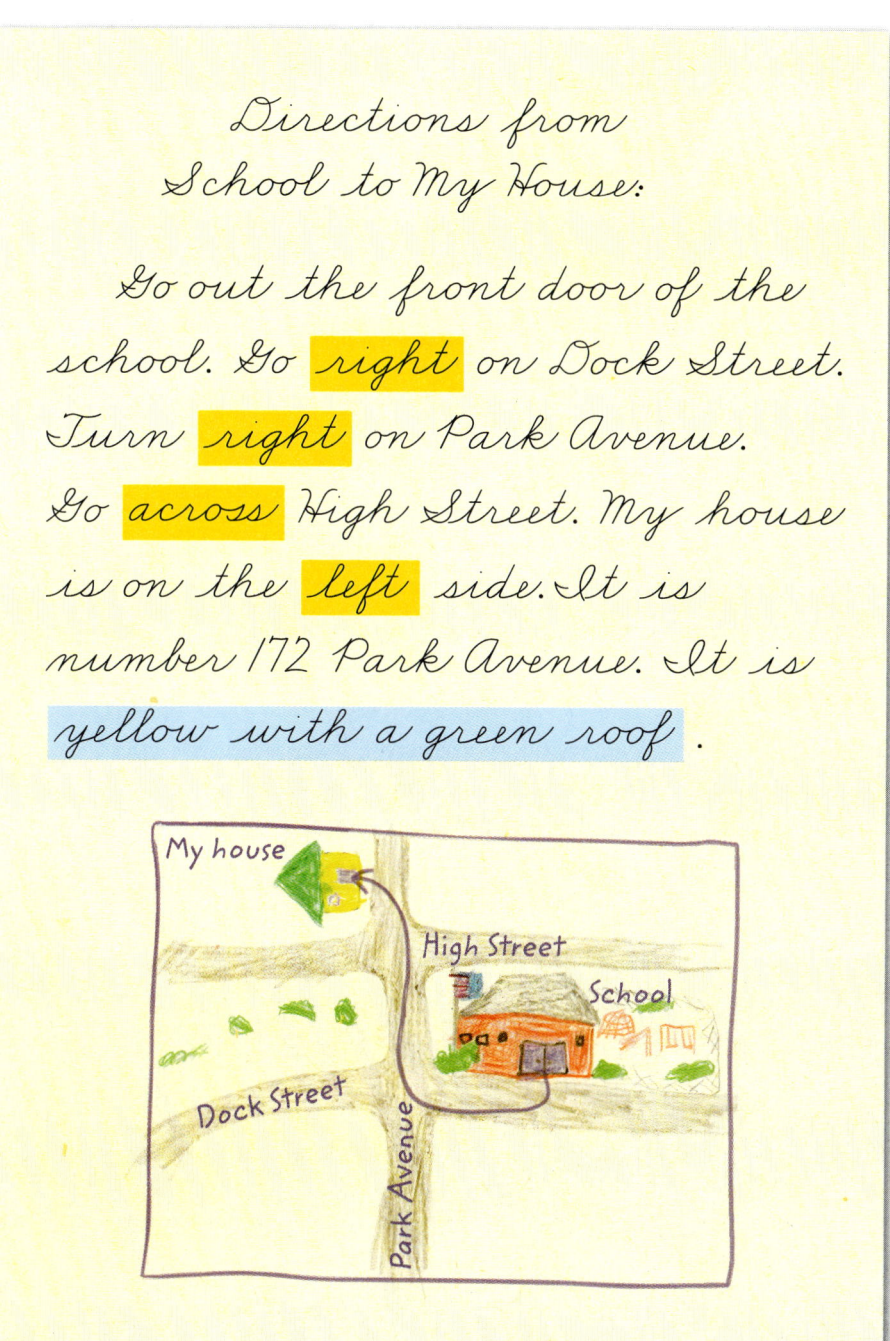

Directions from School to My House:

Go out the front door of the school. Go **right** on Dock Street. Turn **right** on Park Avenue. Go **across** High Street. My house is on the **left** side. It is number 172 Park Avenue. It is **yellow with a green roof**.

Put It in Writing!

E-mail

E-mail is a message you send by computer. "E-mail" is a shorter way to say **electronic mail**. You can send e-mail to anyone who has an e-mail address.

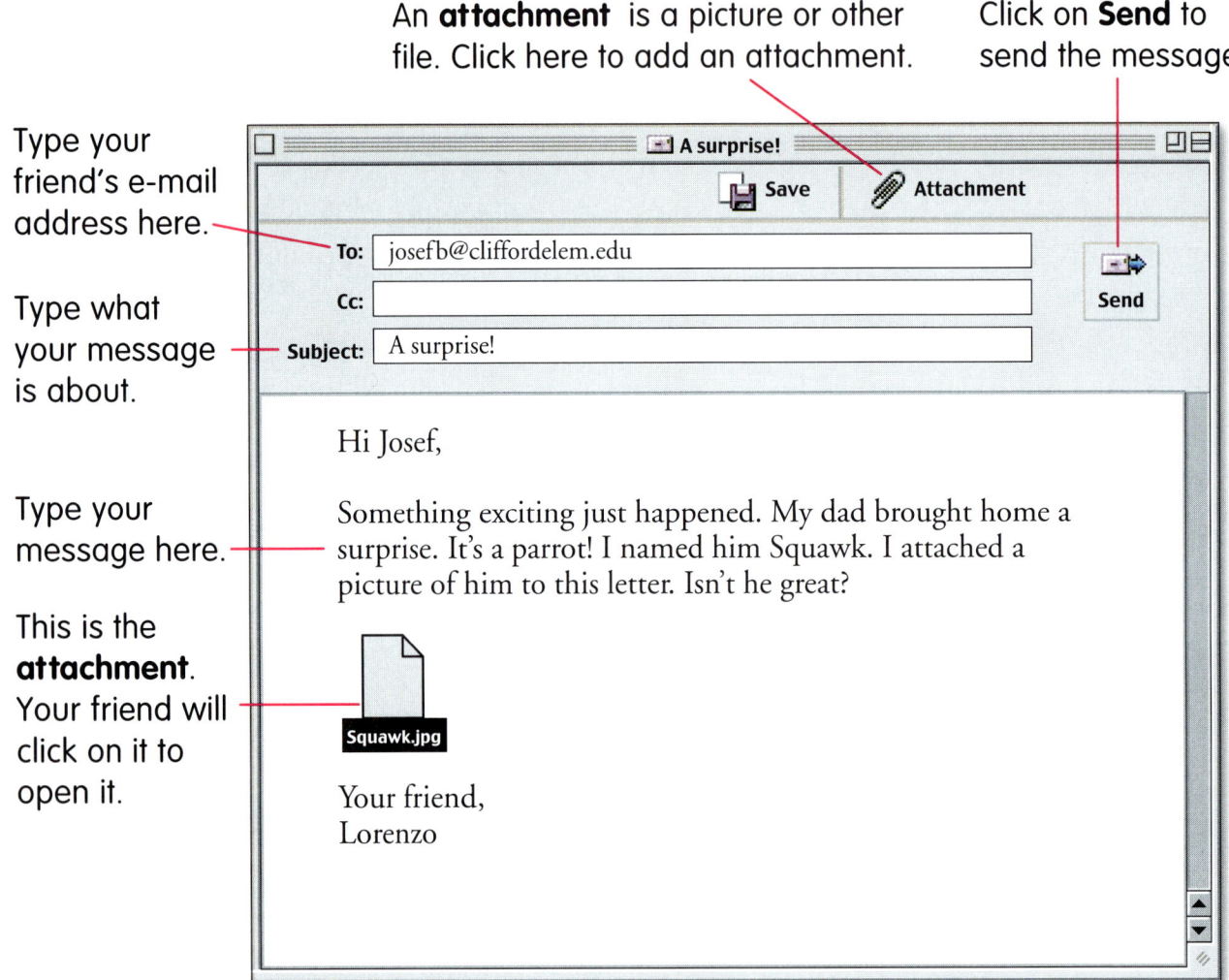

Fable

A **fable** is a story with a lesson, or **moral**. The moral tells what you can learn from the story.

The Ant and the Bird
A Fable by Aesop

An ant and a bird lived in the woods near a stream. One day, the ant wanted a drink. She fell into the stream! The water carried her away.

The bird saw what happened. He dropped a leaf into the stream. Then he yelled, "Crawl onto the leaf!"

The ant crawled onto the leaf. She floated safely to dry land.

Soon, a man came to the woods. He set a trap to catch the bird. The ant stung the man's foot. The man yelled loudly. The bird heard the noise and flew safely away.

Moral: When someone does something nice for you, do something nice back.

The **characters** are often animals. They talk and act like people.

The **moral** comes at the end of the story.

Put It in Writing!

Journal Entry

A **journal** is a special book that you keep for yourself. Each time you write in it, you create a **journal entry**.

Begin with the **date**.

Write about what happened to you.

Tell about your thoughts and feelings.

October 16, 2003

Today Ms. Sims asked us to draw pictures of our favorite things. I drew a dolphin. I thought my picture looked great! Ms. Sims must think it looks great, too. She put it on the wall with a few others. I felt excited and proud. I might draw some more sea animals now, because I like them so much.

Put It in Writing!

Labels and Captions

A **label** names something in a picture.
A **caption** tells more about a picture.

Put It in Writing!

Letters and Notes

Friendly Letter

You can write a **friendly letter** to someone you know well.

8 Red Bird Way
Sacramento, CA 95829
September 9, 2003

Write your address and the date. This is the **heading**.

Write your friend's name in the **greeting**.

Dear Ming,

  I can't believe I have already lived here for two weeks! I like my new school. My teacher asked me to bring in some things that tell about myself. I brought in pictures of you and me at the Golden Dragon parade last year. Now my classmates want to make a giant dragon!
  How is everything in San Francisco? Tell everyone I say hi!

In the **body**, tell your news. Ask questions.

Your friend,
Jin-nah

Write a **closing** and **sign your name**.

132 Put It in Writing!

Envelope

Put your letter in an **envelope**. Write neatly. Check everything carefully. This will help your letter get to the right place!

Write your name and address here. This is the **return address**.

Put a **stamp** in the top right corner.

Write your friend's name and address here. This is the **mailing address**.

Put It in Writing! 133

Invitation

An **invitation** asks someone to come to a party or other special event.

Come to a Kwanzaa Dinner!

Enjoy a special night with family and friends.

Date: Saturday, January 1
Time: 6:30 p.m.
Place: Nikki's house
239 Cook Street

R.S.V.P. 555-0931

Tell **when** and **where** the event will take place.

R.S.V.P. means "Please respond." It asks people to call and say if they will come.

Put It in Writing!

Thank-you Note

Send a **thank-you note** when someone gives you a gift or does something nice for you.

Write the **date**.

Write a **greeting**.

Say "thank you." Tell why you like the gift.

Write a **closing**. Sign your name.

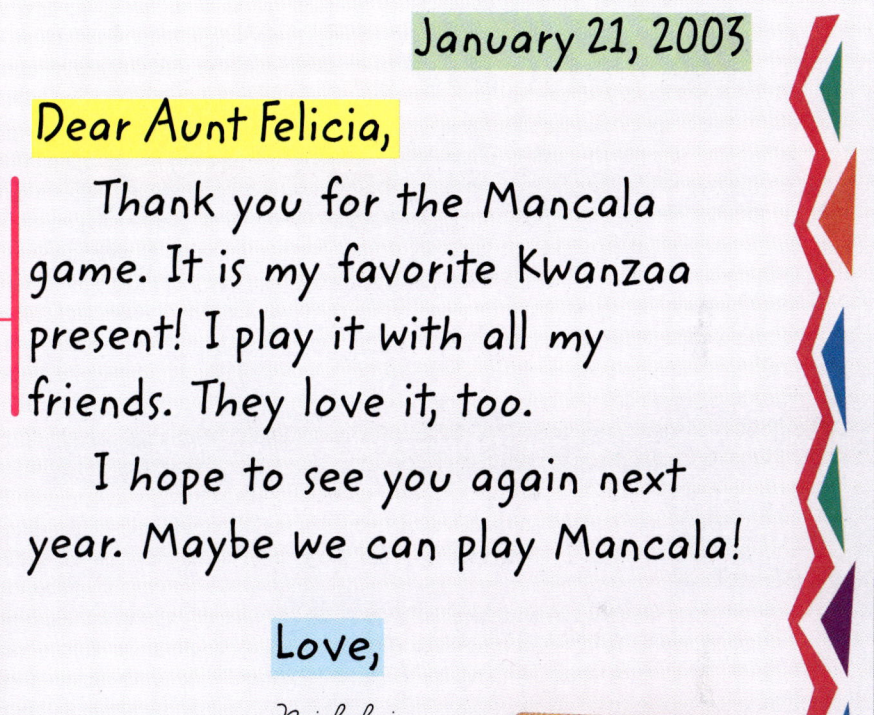

January 21, 2003

Dear Aunt Felicia,

Thank you for the Mancala game. It is my favorite Kwanzaa present! I play it with all my friends. They love it, too.

I hope to see you again next year. Maybe we can play Mancala!

Love,
Nikki

Put It in Writing! 135

Postcard

When you go on a trip, send a **postcard** to your friends. It tells about your trip.

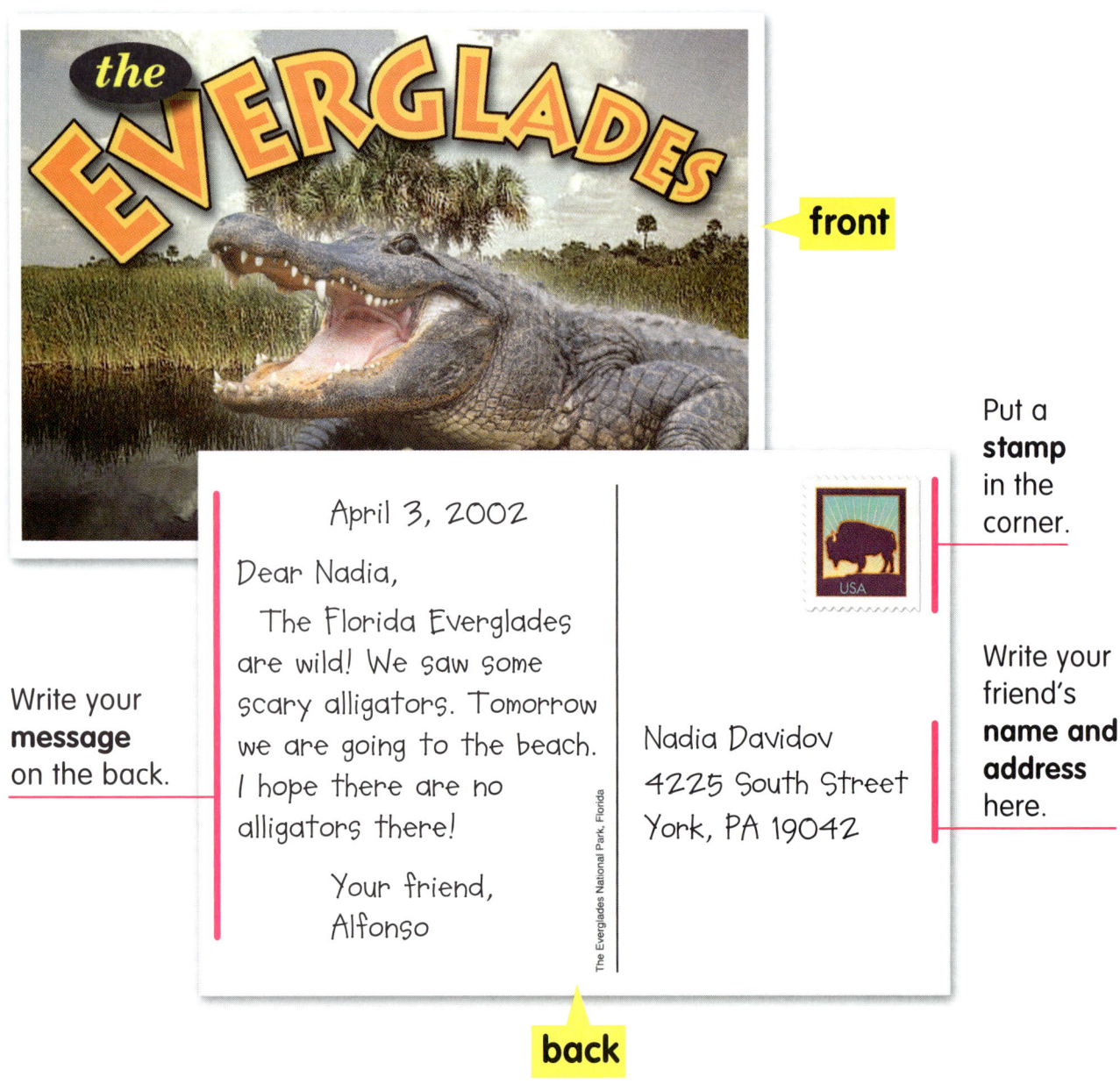

front

Put a **stamp** in the corner.

Write your **message** on the back.

April 3, 2002

Dear Nadia,
   The Florida Everglades are wild! We saw some scary alligators. Tomorrow we are going to the beach. I hope there are no alligators there!

   Your friend,
   Alfonso

Nadia Davidov
4225 South Street
York, PA 19042

Write your friend's **name and address** here.

back

Put It in Writing!

List

A **list** can help you remember things.

Message

A message is a short note. It tells someone something quickly. Here is a **telephone message**.

For whom is the message? Write the name.

Write the date.

Tell who called, when, and why.

Be sure to write the **caller's phone number**.

Sign **your name**.

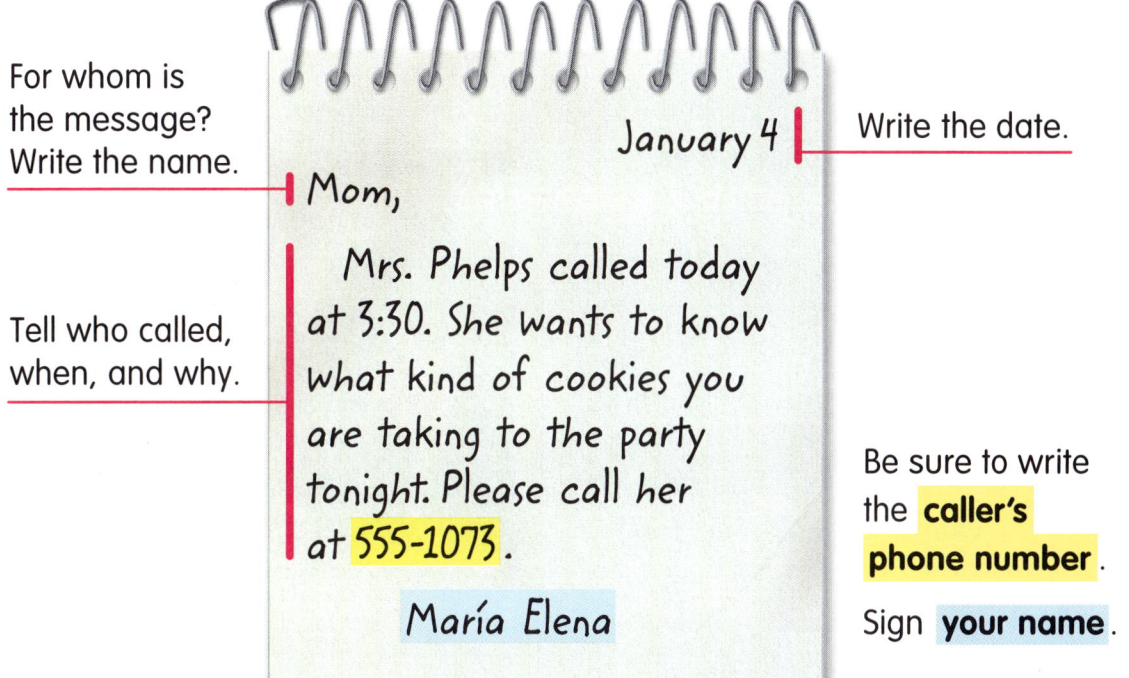

Put It in Writing! 137

Newsletter

A **newsletter** gives information about a school, a club, or another group. Newsletters are often published once a week or once a month.

News Story

A newsletter can have a **news story**. It tells about an event that really happened. It includes **facts**.

The **headline** tells what the story is about.

Facts tell **who**, **what**, **when**, **where**, and **why**.

Pine Street School News
May 2003

Third Graders Clean Up!
by Yolanda Ortiz

Students in Mr. Soto's third-grade class helped clean up City Park last Saturday. They picked up litter and raked leaves. Some students planted flowers. Many parents and teachers helped, too.

Rochelle Lamar is one student who helped. She said, "We wanted to make the park clean and safe. We want it to look nice, too."

Mayor Romero thanked the students. She said, "These students show how we can all work together to make our city better."

Advertisement

A newsletter can have an **advertisement**, or **ad**. An ad tries to get people to buy something. It can include facts and opinions.

An **opinion** tells how someone feels about something.

A **fact** is true information.

Put It in Writing!

Paragraph

A **paragraph** is a group of sentences. They all tell about the same idea. The topic sentence gives the **main idea**. The other sentences give **details** that support it.

A Paragraph with Examples

Some paragraphs give **examples** to support the main idea.

Indent, or leave a space before the first word.

Start with a **topic sentence**. It tells the main idea.

Write detail sentences to give **examples**.

> There are a lot of fun things to do at Jefferson City Park. You can swing on the swings. You can slide down the big slide. You can play basketball or baseball. You can even go to the lake and feed the ducks. That is my favorite thing to do!

Put It in Writing!

Sequence Paragraph

A **sequence paragraph** tells the order, or sequence, of several events. You can write a sequence paragraph to explain how you did something.

The **topic sentence** tells the main thing you did.

The **detail sentences** tell exactly what you did.

Use **time words** and **order words** to show the **sequence**.

Yesterday I helped Mami make salsa. First, we cut up tomatoes, onions, and chiles. Next, we put them in a big bowl. Then we mixed everything together, and the salsa was ready to eat. That night, we had fresh salsa with our steak.

Put It in Writing!

A Paragraph That Compares

When you **compare**, you tell how two or more things are the same or different. You can write a paragraph to compare two people.

The **topic sentence** tells whom you are comparing.

Detail sentences tell how the people are **alike**.

> My brother Elijah looks a lot like my father. They **both** have black, curly hair. Elijah has brown eyes **just like** my father. They have the **same** kind of smile, too! It is very cute. Sometimes I wish that I looked like my father and brother.

Comparison words make your ideas clear.

Put It in Writing!

Opinion Paragraph

In an **opinion paragraph**, you give your thoughts and feelings about a topic.

The topic sentence gives your **opinion**.

The detail sentences give **reasons** for your opinion.

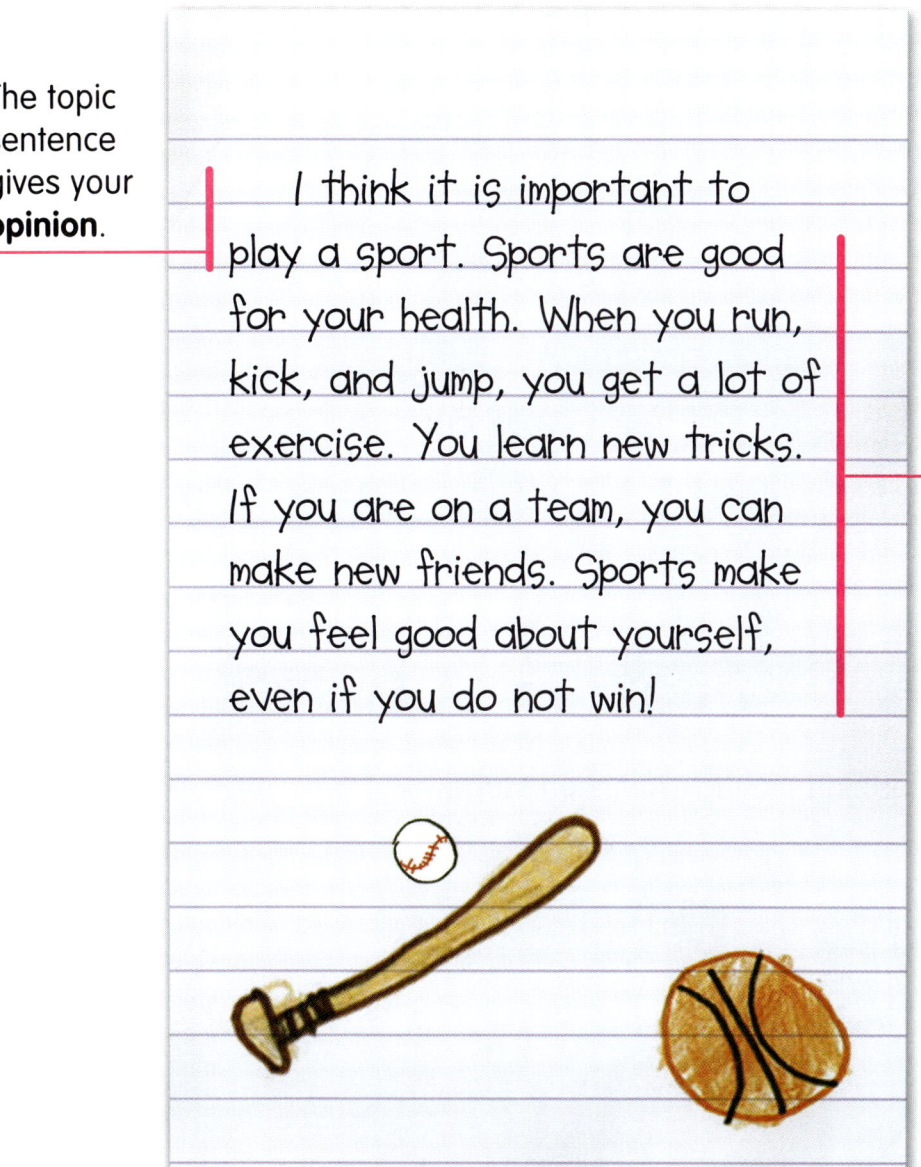

I think it is important to play a sport. Sports are good for your health. When you run, kick, and jump, you get a lot of exercise. You learn new tricks. If you are on a team, you can make new friends. Sports make you feel good about yourself, even if you do not win!

Put It in Writing!

Play

A **play** is a story that is acted out on stage. **Actors** take the roles of the characters. You watch what the actors do, and you listen to what they say.

The actors are performing the play *Annie* **on stage.**

People buy tickets at the **theater** to see the play.

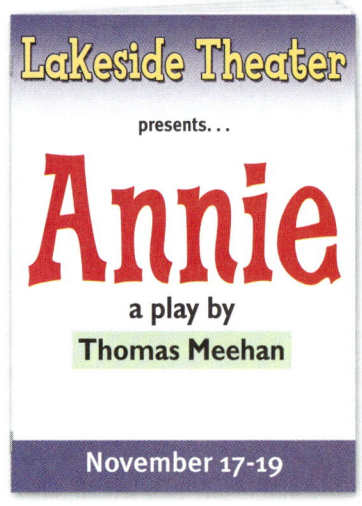

The author of a play is called a **playwright**. The playwright writes the script.

Script for a Play

The **script** tells the actors what to say and do. The actors use the script to **rehearse**, or practice, their lines. Then they perform the play.

The script lists the **characters** and tells the **setting**.

A play often has **acts**. An act is like a chapter in a book. Each act has smaller parts, or **scenes**.

The script shows the **dialogue**, or the words the characters say. The **stage directions** *(in italics)* tell the actors what to do.

Annie

Characters:
Annie, a young girl with no parents
Mr. Warbucks, a rich man
Grace, a woman who works for Mr. Warbucks
Miss Hannigan, a mean woman who runs the home where Annie lives
Other girls who live with Annie

Setting: *New York City in the 1930s*

Act 2, Scene 3

Annie is at Mr. Warbucks' house with Grace.

Grace *(talking to Mr. Warbucks)*: This is Annie. She is the girl you wanted from the orphanage.

Annie: Hello, Mr. Warbucks! It's nice to meet you. *(She holds out her hand to shake his.)*

Mr. Warbucks: I wanted a boy, not a girl! You can't stay.

Put It in Writing! 145

Poem

A **poem** uses words in a special way to give the reader a certain feeling.

Rhyming Poem

In a **rhyming poem**, some of the words **rhyme**, or have the same ending sound. The rhyming words have a **pattern**.

In a poem, a row of words is called a **line**.

Look at the **pattern** in this poem. The **rhyming words** come at the end of every two lines.

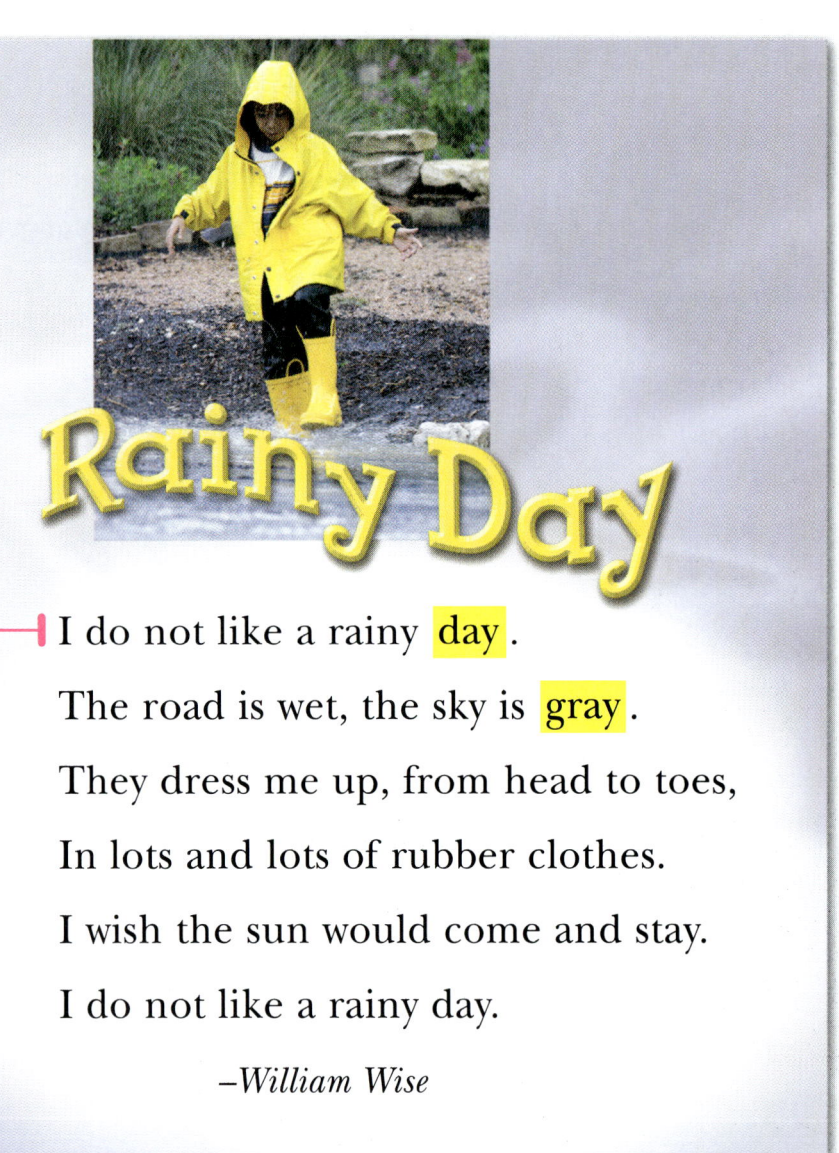

Rainy Day

I do not like a rainy **day**.

The road is wet, the sky is **gray**.

They dress me up, from head to toes,

In lots and lots of rubber clothes.

I wish the sun would come and stay.

I do not like a rainy day.

—William Wise

This poem has rhyming words with a different **pattern**.

Look at the words that **rhyme**. Look at the words that **do not rhyme**. Can you see the **pattern**?

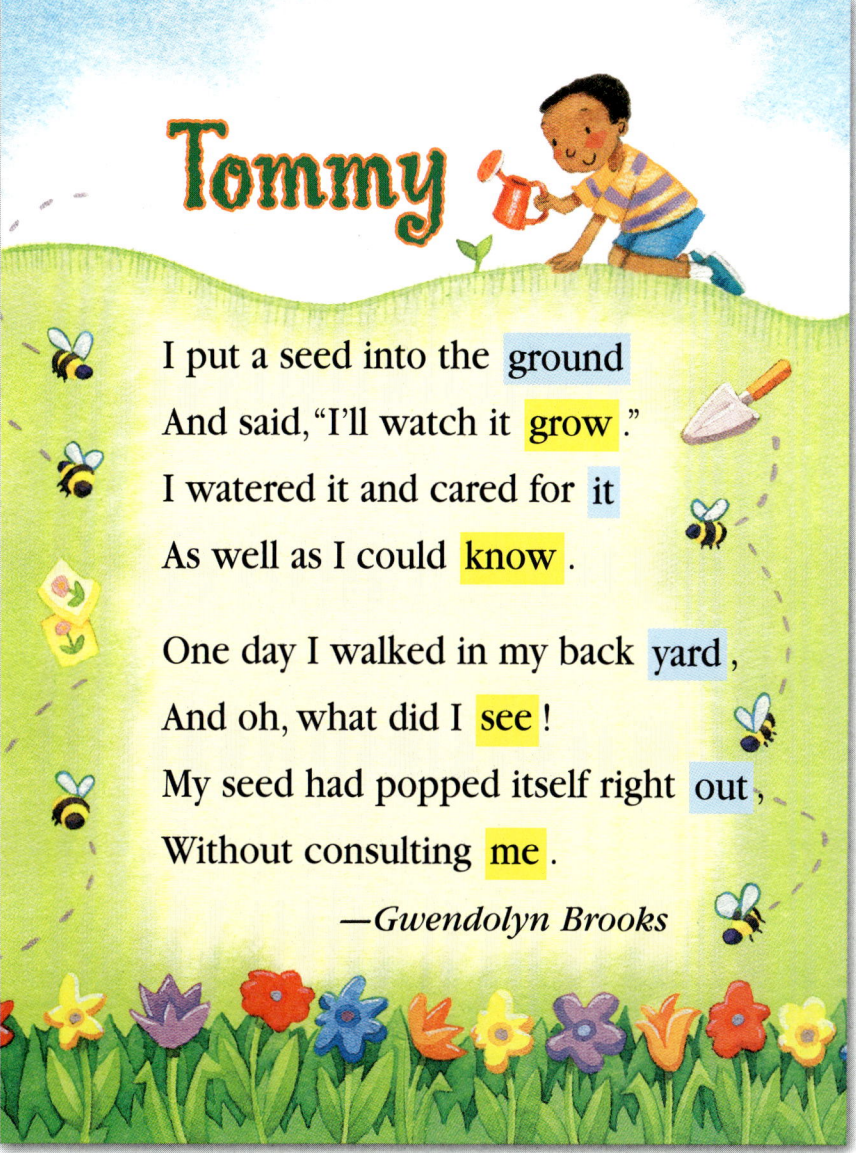

Tommy

I put a seed into the ground
And said, "I'll watch it grow."
I watered it and cared for it
As well as I could know.

One day I walked in my back yard,
And oh, what did I see!
My seed had popped itself right out,
Without consulting me.

—Gwendolyn Brooks

Put It in Writing!

Limerick

A **limerick** is a funny poem with five lines. It has a special pattern. Lines 1, 2, and 5 rhyme one way. Lines 3 and 4 rhyme another way. Lines 1 and 5 sometimes end with the same word.

Chin and **pin** rhyme. **Sharp** and **harp** rhyme.

Lines 3 and 4 are shorter than the others. This gives the poem its **rhythm**, or beat.

There was a young lady whose chin,
Resembled the point of a pin.
So she had it made sharp,
And purchased a harp,
And played several tunes with her chin.

—Edward Lear

Put It in Writing!

Poem with Sound Words

Some poems have words that sound like what they mean. For example, the word **buzz** sounds like the noise a fly makes. These words are called sound words, or **onomatopoeia**.

Say some of the **sound words** out loud. Do they sound like the things they tell about?

Ears Hear

Flies buzz,
Motors roar.
Kettles hiss,
People snore.
Dogs bark,
Birds cheep.
Autos honk: *Beep! Beep!*

Kids shout,
Clocks ding.
Babies cry,
Phones ring.
Balls bounce,
Spoons drop.
People scream: *Stop! Stop!*

—Lucia and James L. Hymes, Jr.

Story

Writers use their imagination to make up stories. These stories are called **fiction**.

- Every story has **characters**. They are the people or animals in the story. In most stories, the characters speak. Their words are called **dialogue**.

Stan and his mother

park rangers

- Every story happens in a certain place and time. This is called the **setting**.

the beach on Saturday

- Every story has a **plot**. The plot tells what events happen in the **beginning**, **middle**, and **end** of a story.

beginning

middle

end

Put It in Writing!

Realistic Fiction

Realistic fiction tells about events that can really happen.

The Little Lost Whale
by Ari Graff

Stan and his mother went to the beach on Saturday. They saw a baby whale. It was almost up to the beach.

"We have to help the baby whale!" cried Stan. "It must be lost!"

Stan and his mom called the park rangers. The rangers came with a raft. They worked for a long time. Finally the rangers got the baby whale away from shore. The whale swam out to sea.

Stan was happy. "I bet that little whale will be glad to see his mother," said Stan. He hugged his own mother tightly.

The **characters** and **setting** seem real. These **events** could really happen.

These **events** could really happen.

Put It in Writing!

Fantasy

A **fantasy** is a story about things that could never happen in real life.

RABBIT, COYOTE, AND THE BIG ROCK

A Folk Tale from Guatemala

One day, Rabbit was leaning on a big rock when Coyote came by. Rabbit decided to play a trick on Coyote.

"What are you doing?" Coyote asked Rabbit.

"Help me, Coyote! The sky is falling on us! Lean against this rock to hold up the sky. I'll go get a stick," said Rabbit. "We can use it to keep the rock up."

"All right," said Coyote. He leaned against

In real life, animals cannot talk. In this **fantasy**, Rabbit and Coyote talk to each other.

Put It in Writing!

the rock with all his might.

Rabbit ran off and left Coyote holding up the rock. After a while, Coyote shouted, "Hurry up, Rabbit! I'm getting very tired." Rabbit did not come back.

A little later, Coyote cried, "Rabbit, WHERE ARE YOU? I can't hold up this rock any longer!" Rabbit still did not come back. Finally Coyote decided to leave. "I don't care if the sky falls down," he said.

As Coyote was running away, he fell into a ravine! That's how Coyote was lost forever, and Rabbit never did come back.

In a **fantasy**, the characters often do things they cannot do in real life. Here Coyote holds up a rock.

Put It in Writing!

A Story About You

You can write a story about something that happened to you. This kind of story is called a **personal narrative**.

Use **I**, **me** and **my**. They show that the story is about you.

My Visit to Japan

When I was three years old, my family moved to the U.S. from Japan. This year, my parents took me back to Japan for the first time. I was very excited. I wanted to see my grandparents. I also wanted to see Tokyo, where I was born.

My grandparents met us at the airport. We hugged and hugged. I felt so happy! They said I looked much bigger than before. I laughed. I look the same to me!

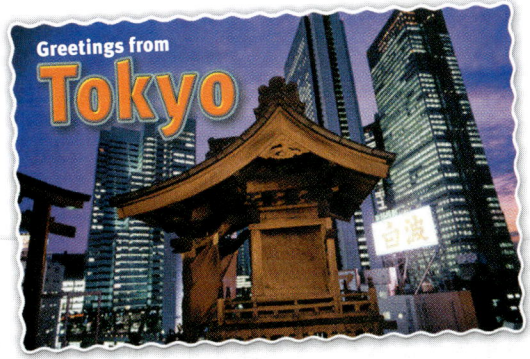

Then my grandparents took us to Tokyo. When I saw the city, I was surprised. There were so many cars and people and signs. I did not remember any of that!

Now we are back from Japan. I am happy because I have two countries to love—Japan and the United States.

Tell what happened to you. Tell how you felt about it.

Put It in Writing!

Summary

In a **summary**, you tell about something you have read or seen. You write only the most important ideas. Read this article.

Corn Pops Up Everywhere!

What plant is used to make food, medicine, and fuel? What plant grows all over the world? The answer is corn!

Scientists think that thousands of years ago, native people of the Americas grew a corn plant that was good to eat. Explorers took the plant back to Europe. Corn farming spread quickly around the world after that.

One reason corn became so popular is that it grows well almost anywhere. It can grow in the mountains or by the sea. It can grow in rainy places and in dry places.

Corn is an important food. People eat cornbread, popcorn, and corn tortillas. Animals eat a lot of corn, too! Most of the corn grown in the U.S. is for cows, pigs, and other farm animals.

Corn is also used to make products such as glue, ink, and some medicines. There is even a fuel for cars made from corn. It helps gasoline burn better so there is less pollution.

Corn is very helpful!

Put It in Writing!

Follow these steps to write a summary of the article:

1 Make a list of the most important ideas. These are the **main ideas**.

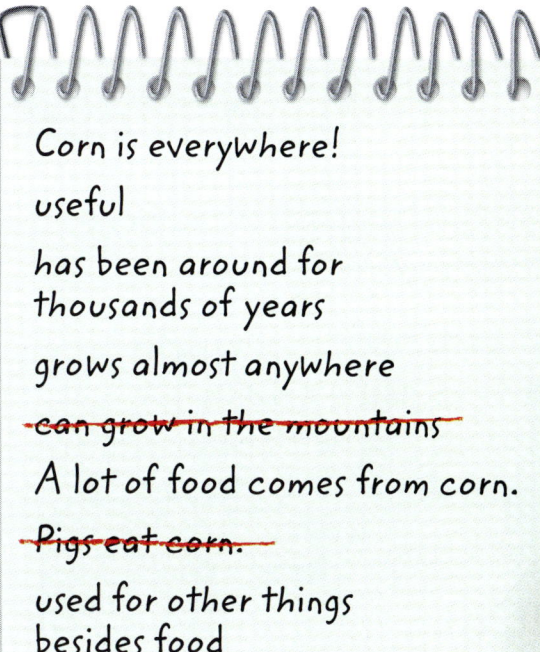

2 Read through your list. Cross out details. Keep only the main ideas.

3 Turn your notes into sentences. Use your own words.

> People have been growing corn for thousands of years. It is very useful, and it can grow almost anywhere. A lot of food is made from corn. Corn is used to make other products, too. Corn is very important!

Put It in Writing!

The Good Writer Guide

How to Collect Ideas

To be a good writer, you need ideas. You can collect ideas from many places.

■ **Look! Listen!** Pay attention everywhere you go. Take notes about what you hear. Draw what you see.

■ **Read!** Read books, magazines, and newspapers. Search the Internet. When you read:

- list fun facts.
- write down words you like.
- draw your favorite characters.
- write questions.
- list topics that you want to learn more about.

■ **Brainstorm!** Think about a subject. What do you already know about it? What ideas can you get from other people? You can make a web to collect ideas.

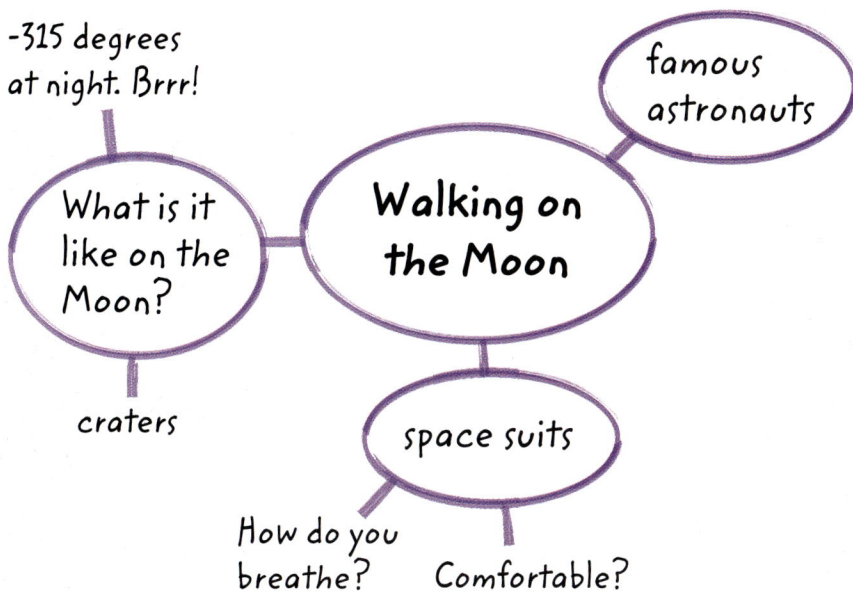

■ **Save Your Ideas.** You may use them later.

You can write ideas in a **notebook**.

You can write ideas on cards. Put them in a **file box**.

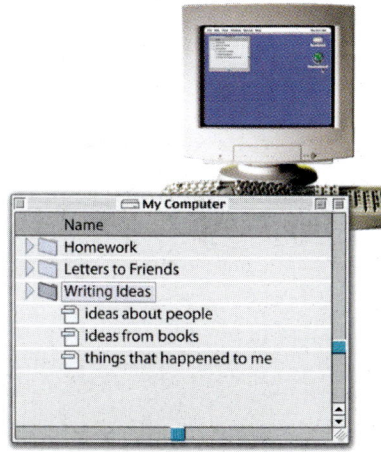

You can save ideas on a **computer**.

Put It in Writing! 159

How to Write for a Purpose

Why are you writing? That is your reason, or **purpose**. There are many different purposes for writing.

1 You can **give information**. You can explain or tell facts about something. You can tell how to do something.

> The Saguaro
> The saguaro is a cactus plant that grows in hot, dry places. It has thick skin and prickly needles. Its long arms, or branches, reach up toward the sky.

2 You can **express yourself**. You can express your thoughts and feelings to other people. You can also write in a journal, just for you.

> February 1, 2003
>
> Today Aunt Camila is coming to visit. She is flying all the way from Costa Rica! I can't wait to see her.

3. You can **record ideas**. Write down things you want to remember. Tell what you think about something, such as a character in a story.

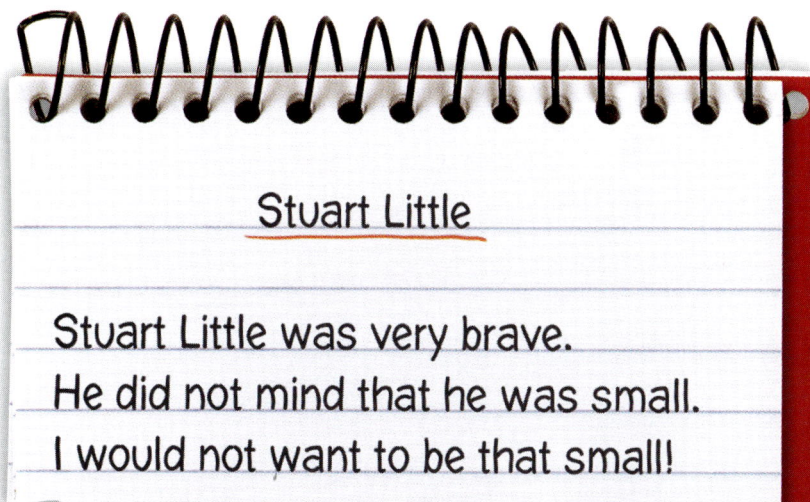

4. You can **invite someone**. You can ask the person to come to a special event. Tell the time and place of the event.

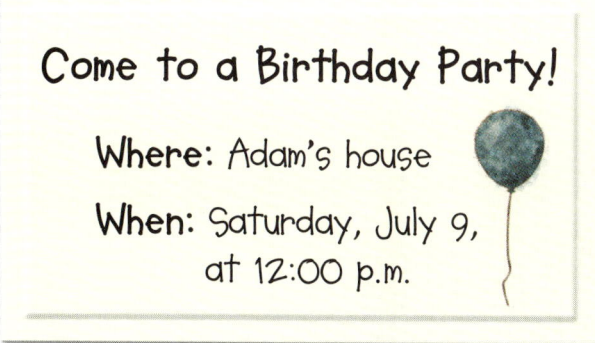

How to Write for a Purpose, continued

5 You can **describe**. You can tell what someone or something is like.

> ### The Old Barn
> Daria slowly opened the door to the old barn. It was dark inside. Only a little bit of light came in through a small window. The air was cold. It smelled like wet straw. Daria shivered. Suddenly, she heard a tiny squeak!

6 You can **write to learn**. Write things down to remember them better, to discover new things, and to develop new ideas.

> What I learned from Sophie's report:
>
> - Kinds of storms: hurricane, blizzard, typhoon
>
> - A hurricane can have winds up to 160 miles per hour!

7 You can **entertain people**. You can write something that people will enjoy reading.

> Lunch
> My friend made me a sandwich.
> She started with some bread.
> She spread some jam,
> Then added ham.
> "YOU eat it," I said!

8 You can **thank someone**. Tell how much you like a gift you received or something that a person did.

> July 14, 2003
>
> Dear Ramesh,
>   Thank you for coming to my party. I like the baseball cap you gave me. The Padres are my favorite team! I will wear the cap all the time.
>
>   See you soon!
>   Adam

Put It in Writing!

Choose a Form for Your Purpose

Once you know your purpose for writing, choose a writing form. For example:

■ If you want to **give information,** you could write:

How Tadpoles Become Frogs

Tadpoles hatch from eggs. In a few months, the tadpoles grow into adult frogs.

a report

Dear Hakeem,

Guess what! I found out that tadpoles can turn into frogs in two or three months!

a letter

■ If you want to **describe something** you could write:

Dear Jesse,

My new baby sister is so cute! Her skin is really soft.

a letter

My baby sister has
Soft, dark skin,
And a little dimple
On her chin.

a poem

Put It in Writing!

- If you want to **entertain people**, you could write:

  Jack: Mom! I sold the cow and got these magic beans!
  Jack's mom *(very angry)*: BEANS? You got BEANS?

  a play script

  Jack climbed the stalk that grew from the beans. He climbed and climbed, Till he ripped his jeans!

  a poem

- If you want to **express yourself**, you could write:

  Friday, August 7

  I'm so happy. Dad says I can keep the stray kitten! I think I will name her Lucky because that's how I felt when I found her.

  a journal entry

  Lucky

  When I got home from school yesterday, I found a surprise on the doorstep. It was a tiny kitten. She looked hungry and scared.

  a story about you

Put It in Writing!

How to Write for Your Audience

The people who read what you write are your **audience**. When you write, think about what your audience needs to know. Write in a way that fits your audience.

- For **adults or people you don't know**, use formal language. Include **details** your audience may not know.

> My classmates and I have swimming lessons every Tuesday. We go to the pool at the YMCA. Our last swimming lesson was the best. We learned how to swim underwater.

- For **your family**, write the way you talk. Leave out details your family already knows.

> Swimming was great! I can swim underwater now. I'll tell you all about it at dinner.

Put It in Writing!

- For **your friends**, write the way you talk to them. Use informal words. Tell about things that will interest your friends.

> My swimming lesson was awesome! I finally learned how to swim underwater. Paolo and Elizabeth were there, too. They are the best swimmers!

- For **younger children**, use simple words that children will know. You may want to draw a picture, too.

> My swimming lesson was fun! Now I can swim underwater. My friends helped me.

Put It in Writing!

How to Choose Words

Good writers read their writing many times. Each time, they work on it to make it better. Try these ways to make your writing sparkle!

Use Precise Words

Words that are **precise** make your writing clearer. They tell exactly what you mean. Use precise words to name people, places, and things.

Just OK

> She got her things. She put them in a bag. Then she looked around the room.

Much better!

> Tran got her jacket and soccer ball. She put them in a bag. Then she looked around her bedroom.

The writer used **precise words** to tell exactly **who**, **what**, and **where**.

Use Vivid Words

Vivid means "colorful" or "full of feeling." Vivid words help readers see, hear, taste, feel, or smell what is happening.

Just OK

Tran got her jacket and soccer ball. She put them in a bag. Then she looked around her bedroom.

Much better!

Tran **grabbed** her **fuzzy, red** jacket and soccer ball. She **stuffed** them in a **big** bag. Then she looked around her **messy** bedroom.

The writer used **vivid words** to give a clear picture.

You can use a special book, called a **thesaurus**, to find precise and vivid words.

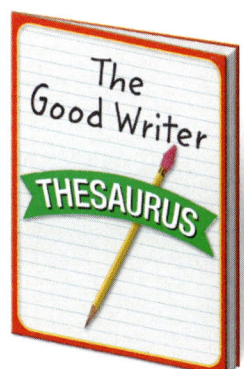

Put It in Writing!

How to Use a Thesaurus

A **thesaurus** is a special kind of book. It lists synonyms and antonyms for words.

- **Synonyms** mean almost the same thing.

    little, small

- **Antonyms** mean the opposite.

    little, big

Writers often use a thesaurus to find a vivid word.

To find a vivid word for **big**:

1. Look up the word **big** in the thesaurus. The words are listed in alphabetical order. Look at the **guide words** to help you find the page where **big** appears.

2. Look down the list of **entry words** until you see **big**. Find the synonyms.

   > **big** The word **big** tells about the size of something.
   > **Synonyms** large, huge, enormous
   > **Antonyms** small, tiny, little

3. Choose the synonym that best describes what you want to say.

   > She stuffed them in a ~~big~~ huge bag.

Put It in Writing!

This **guide word** matches the **first word** on the **left page**.

This **guide word** matches the **last word** on the **right page**.

baby

baby A **baby** is a very young child or animal.
  Synonyms infant, child
  Antonyms adult, grown-up

bad Something that is **bad** is something you do not like. It can also be something you should not do.
  Synonyms awful, horrible, terrible
  Antonyms good, great

beat When you **beat** a drum, you hit it to make a sound.
  Synonyms hit, pound, strike

entry word

big

beautiful Something that looks or sounds very nice is **beautiful**.
  Synonyms pretty, lovely
  Antonym ugly

below **Below** means to be lower than something else.
  Synonyms beneath, under
  Antonyms above, over

big The word **big** tells about the size of something.
  Synonyms large, huge, enormous
  Antonyms small, tiny, little

The elephant is **big**.

28   29

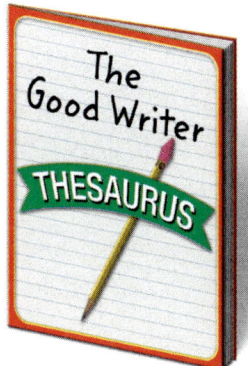

Put It in Writing! 171

How to Write Better Sentences

Write Complete Sentences

A sentence begins with a **capital letter**. It has an **end mark**.

Examples: **T**he soccer game is today**.**
What time does the game begin**?**
We do not want to be late**!**

A sentence tells a complete thought.

Not OK Her mother.

OK Her mother waited downstairs.

Not OK ran out of her room

OK Tran ran out of her room.

Put It in Writing!

Combine Short Sentences

Too many short sentences can sound choppy. Combine them into longer sentences.

Just OK

Tran ran out of her room.
Tran ran down the stairs.

Better

Tran ran out of her room **and** down the stairs.

You can use the word **and** to join two sentences.

Just OK

Tran forgot the bag. Tran ran upstairs to get it.

Better

Tran forgot the bag **and** ran upstairs to get it.

Put It in Writing! 173

How to Write Better Sentences, continued

Fix Run-on Sentences

A **run-on** sentence uses the word **and** too many times. Turn a run-on sentence into two sentences.

Not OK

> Tran forgot the bag upstairs and she ran up the stairs to get it and she raced back down the stairs.

OK

> Tran forgot the bag and ran upstairs to get it. Then she raced back down the stairs.

or

> Tran forgot the bag upstairs. She ran up the stairs to get it and then raced back down the stairs.

Put It in Writing!

Use Different Kinds of Sentences

When you write, include **statements, questions,** and **exclamations**. A good mix makes your writing more interesting.

> Tran grabbed her fuzzy, red jacket and soccer ball. She stuffed them in a huge bag. Then she looked around her messy bedroom. Her mother waited downstairs. Tran ran out of her room and down the stairs. ~~Tran forgot the bag and~~ Oh no! Where was the bag? It was still in her room! Tran ran upstairs to get it. Then she raced back down the stairs.

Put It in Writing!

How to Add Details

Details make your writing more interesting. You can add details to tell **what**, **when**, **where**, and **how**.

Just OK

> Tran loved to play soccer. She wanted to be on a soccer team. Tran practiced a lot. Soon she was good.

Much better!

> Tran loved to play soccer. She wanted to be on <mark>the school</mark> soccer team. <mark>Every day</mark> Tran <mark>went to the park</mark> and practiced. Soon she was good <mark>enough to join the team</mark>.

Put It in Writing!

Show, Don't Tell

Use **actions** to show how a character feels or thinks. Use **dialogue**, or a person's words, to show what the character is like.

This tells

> The game was close. Tran felt nervous and excited. She wanted the coach to put her in the game. Tran was ready to play.

This shows

> The score was tied. There was only one minute left. Tran ==couldn't stand still==.
>
> "Please give me a chance, Coach!" Tran begged. "I know I can do it!"
>
> "Yes, I think you're ready. You've scored a lot of goals in practice," he answered.

Tran's **actions** show that she is nervous and excited. Tran's words, or **dialogue**, show that she tries hard and does not give up.

Put It in Writing! 177

Review Your Writing

■ **Save** your writing in a **portfolio** so you can review it often. A portfolio is a place to save special papers.

folder file

big envelopes

notebook

■ **Sort** your writing in groups that make sense to you.

Put your writing in the order that it was written.

Or, keep the same kinds of writing together.

■ **Think about your writing.** Read the writing in your portfolio. Think about what you did well. Set goals for how you can make your writing better. Ask yourself:

- ✓ What is my best piece of writing? Why?
- ✓ How has my writing changed?
- ✓ What can I do to make my writing better?
- ✓ What other kinds of writing do I want to try?

I like my story about the soccer game. It has a funny ending.

I will learn to use a thesaurus. Then my words will be more vivid.

I want to write funny poems.

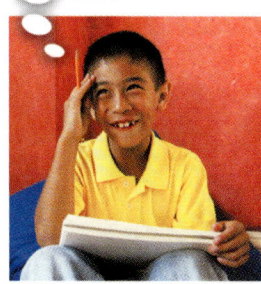

Put It in Writing! 179

Chapter 4
Present It!

Life in El Salvador

You have something important to say! Learn how to present ideas when you speak and write. Then people will get the idea!

Read Aloud

One way to **present**, or share, a story is to read it out loud to others.

Read-Aloud Tips

- ✓ Read loudly and clearly enough for everyone to hear.
- ✓ Make your voice sound like what is happening in the story.
- ✓ Stop for a moment after a very exciting or important part.
- ✓ Show the pictures.

Present It!

Listen to a Story

When you listen to someone read a book, listen to understand and enjoy the story.

Listening Tips

- ✓ Make a picture of the story in your mind.
- ✓ Look at the pictures in the book.
- ✓ Pay attention to the reader's voice and face.
- ✓ Remember to have fun!

"The wolf tumbled down, down, and bumped his head."

Present It!

Give a Message

A **message** is information that one person gives to another person. When you give a message, you give information that the person needs to know.

Speaking Tips

✓ Get your listeners' attention.

✓ Make your message as simple as possible.

✓ Check to see if your message is understood.

✓ Repeat your message if necessary.

The library closes in five minutes.

Present It!

Get a Message

When you get a message, listen carefully. Show that you understand the message.

Okay, I understand.

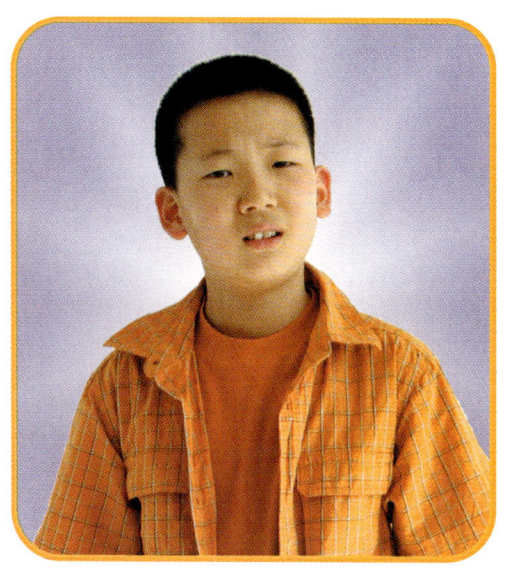

I do not understand.

That's great!

I am surprised!

Present It!

Give a Talk

To tell information about a topic, you can give a talk.

Speaking Tips

✓ Think about what you will say. Make **notes**.

✓ Think about who will listen to your talk. They are your **audience**.

Your Audience	How to Speak to Them
Friends	Talk as you usually do.
Younger children	Use easier words.
Parents and teachers	Use formal language.

✓ Practice your talk.

✓ Make charts and pictures.

✓ Show the real things if you can. These are called **props**.

✓ Look at your audience.

Listen to a Talk

When you are in the **audience**, listen to get information.

Listening Tips
- ✓ Look at the speaker.
- ✓ Sit quietly.
- ✓ Listen carefully.
- ✓ Look at charts and pictures.
- ✓ Pay attention to details.
- ✓ Raise your hand to ask a question.

audience

Present It!

Talk in a Group

When you have a **discussion**, you talk in a group. People in the group take turns speaking and listening.

Speaking Tips
- Talk only about the topic.
- Ask questions.
- Take turns.
- If you do not know how to say something one way, try another way.

I like the story. It's funny. I laughed at the end.

Listen in a Group

When you are part of a discussion, listen to learn what others think.

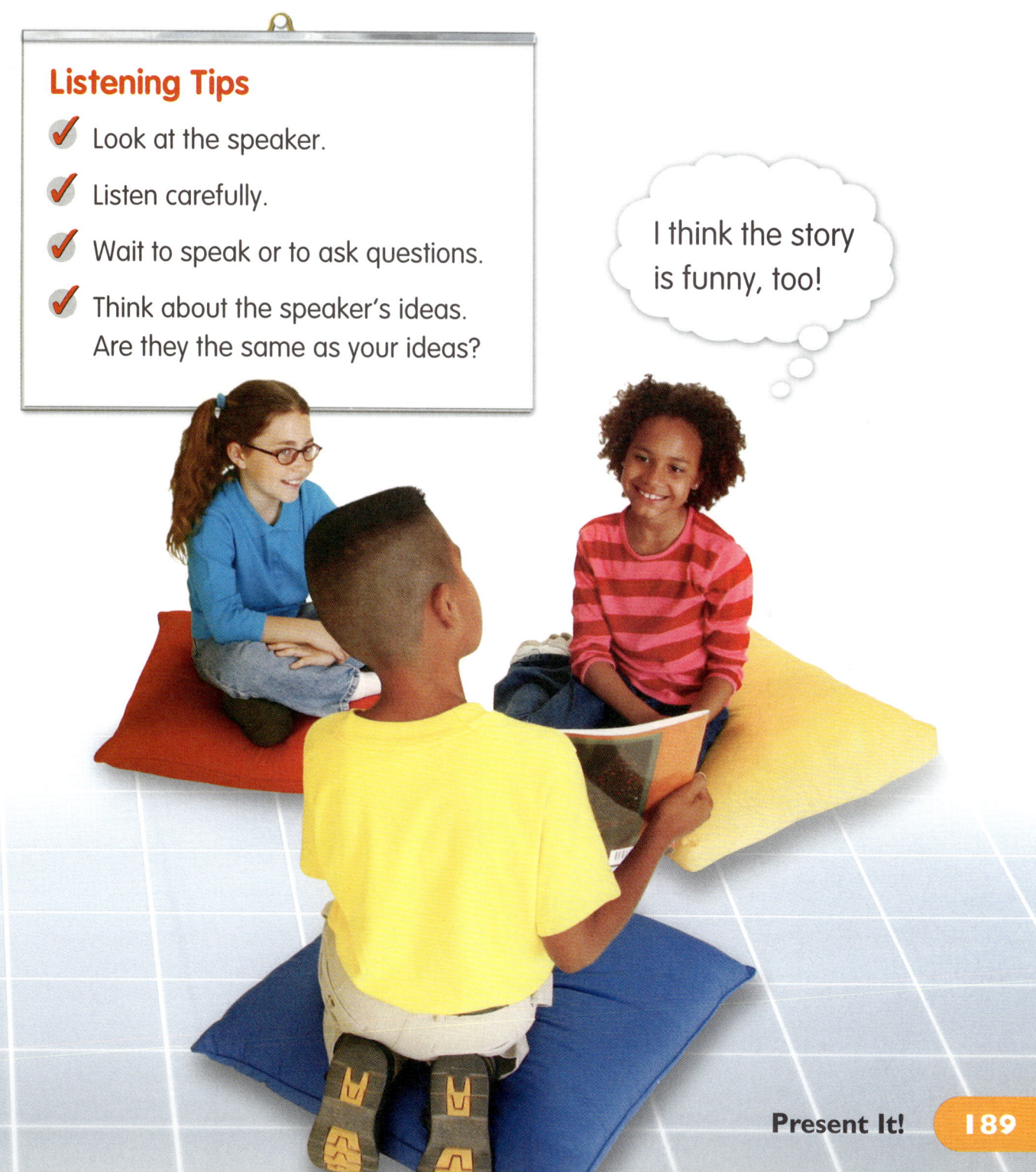

Listening Tips
- ✓ Look at the speaker.
- ✓ Listen carefully.
- ✓ Wait to speak or to ask questions.
- ✓ Think about the speaker's ideas. Are they the same as your ideas?

I think the story is funny, too!

Present It!

Find and Make Pictures

Pictures can help you tell about ideas and information.

Where to Find Pictures

Cut pictures from old magazines and newspapers.

Print pictures from the Internet.

Look for pictures in books.

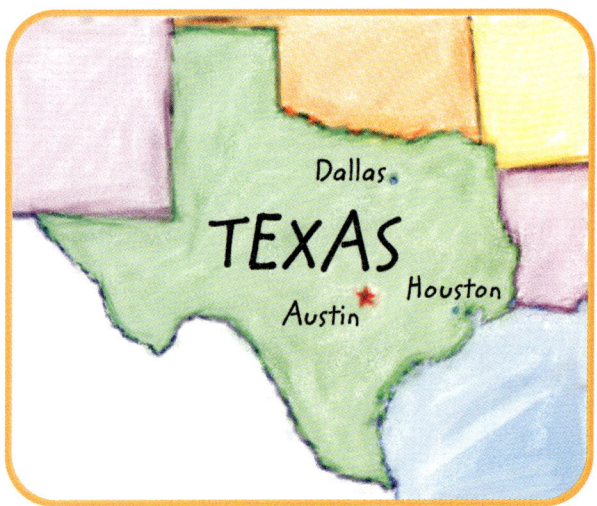

Create your own diagrams, graphs, and maps.

Present It!

When to Use Pictures

Use pictures for reports, announcements, and talks.

Tips for Using Pictures

- Use photographs to show how something real looks.
- Draw pictures to show details.
- Use diagrams, charts, and maps to help explain things.

View Pictures

When you look at pictures, think about **why** you are looking at them.

Look at pictures to **understand** more about something.

Look at pictures to **learn how** to make or do something.

Look at pictures to **have fun**!

My dog is so cute!

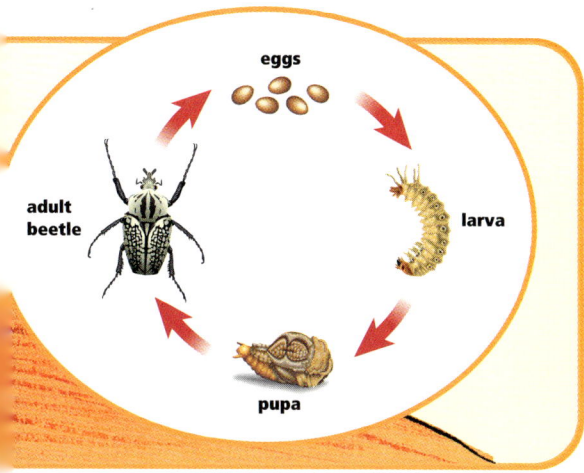

Viewing Tips

✓ Look at details in photographs. Notice color, shape, and size.

The legs are long. There are six.

The body is black and yellow.

✓ When you look at diagrams, see how parts work together.

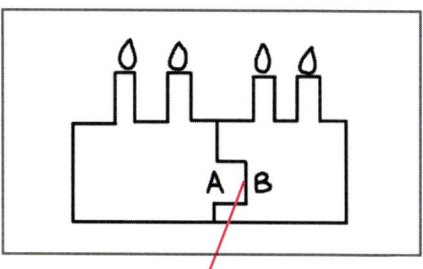

The ends go together here.

✓ When you look at maps, notice where things are.

Here is the pet store.

Present It!

Handwriting and Spelling Guide

Make sure your audience can read your work. Use your best handwriting, or **penmanship**, and spell each word correctly.

Get Ready to Write

Good handwriting starts with how you sit at your desk and hold your pencil.

Hold your pencil this way.

Sit up straight.

Put both feet on the floor.

If you are left-handed:

If you are right-handed:

194 Present It!

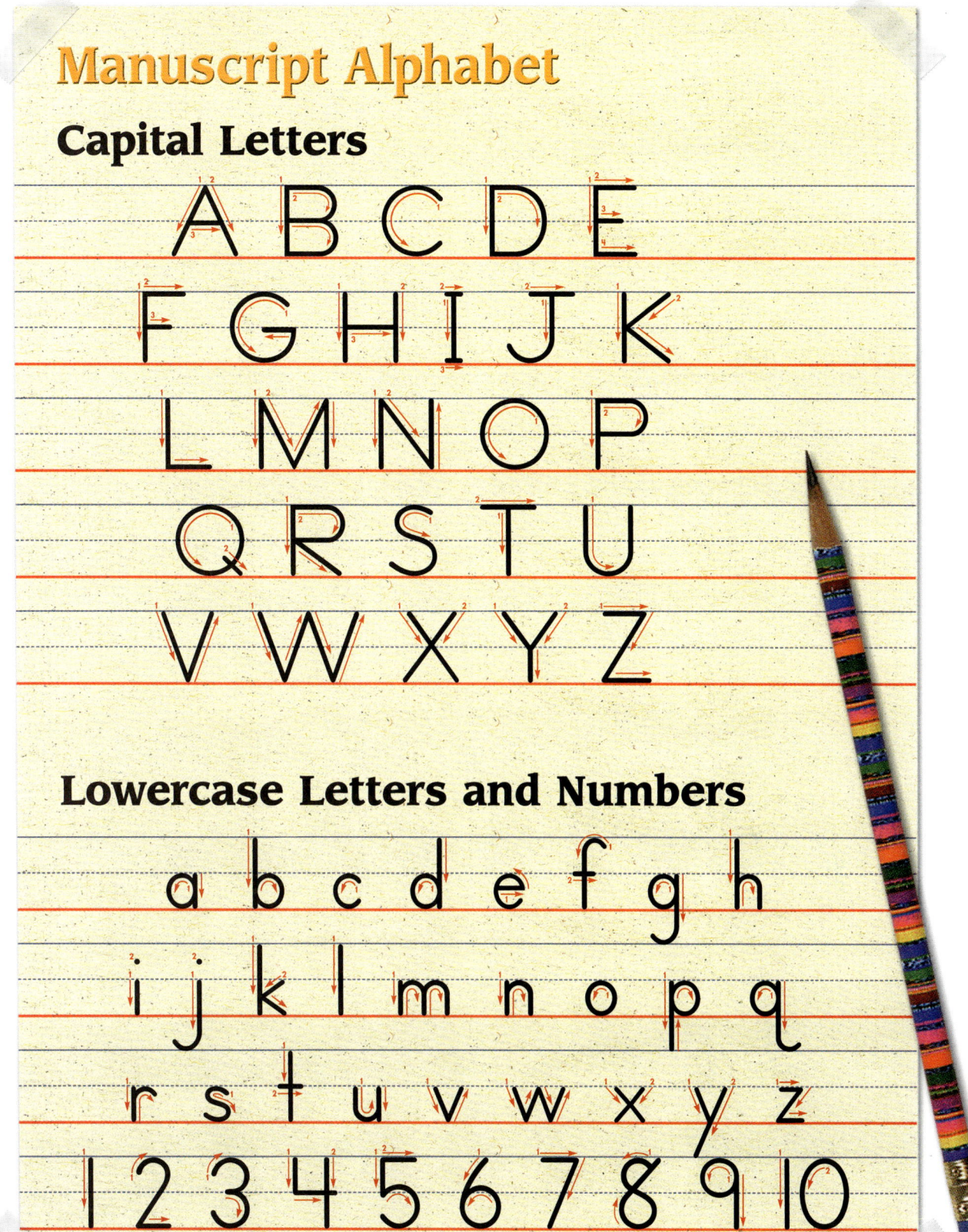

Write Letters

- Make letters the **right size**.

Not OK	Not OK	OK

too big	too small	

- Make letters the **right shape**.

Not OK	Not OK	OK

- Put the **right amount of space** between the letters in a word.

Not OK	Not OK	OK

too far	too close	

Present It!

Write Words and Sentences

- Start each sentence with a capital letter.
- End each sentence with an end mark.

Not OK

today I went to the zoo

should be a capital letter   *needs a period*

OK

Today I went to the zoo.

- Put more space between words than between letters.
- Put the same amount of space between each word.

Not OK

I sawa sleepy   bear.

not enough space   *too much space*

OK

I saw a sleepy bear.

Present It!

Write Sentences in a Paragraph

- **Indent**, or leave a space, at the beginning of each paragraph.

- Leave blank spaces, or **margins**, on the top, bottom, left, and right of your writing.

- Leave more space between sentences than between words.

Indent each paragraph.

Start your writing at the left **margin**.

    Alligators are reptiles that live in marshes and swamps. They have tough skin, short legs, and long tails. Their large jaws have many sharp teeth.

198   **Present It!**

Cursive Alphabet

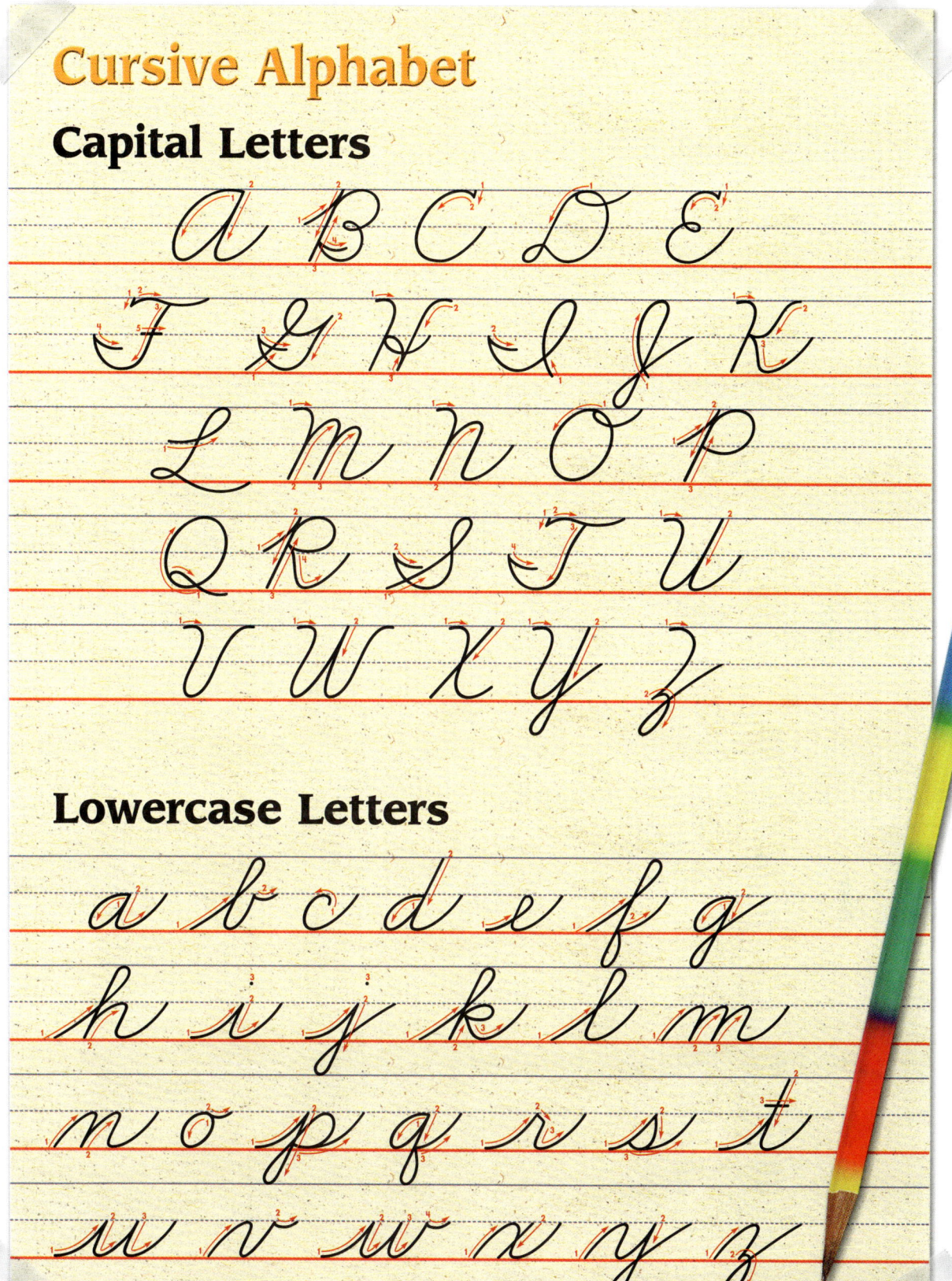

Present It! 199

Write Words

■ **Connect** the letters.

      Not OK   Not OK   OK

 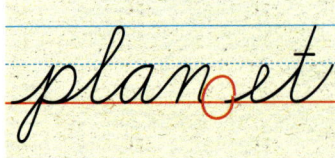 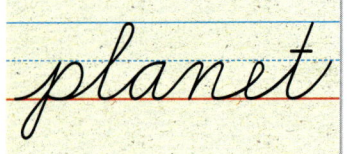

■ Make letters the **right size and shape**.

      Not OK   Not OK   OK

  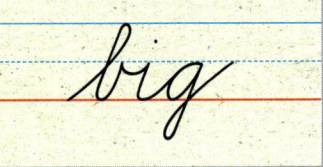

■ Do not put letters too far apart or too close together.

      Not OK   Not OK   OK

too far   too close

Present It!

Write Sentences

■ Put a space between words.

Not OK

Earth goesaround thesun.

should be a space

OK

Earth goes around the sun.

■ Make sure your letters sit on the bottom line.

Not OK

Earth also spins.

should be on the bottom line

OK

Earth also spins.

Present It!

Write Sentences in a Paragraph

- **Indent**, or leave a space, at the beginning of each paragraph.

- Leave blank spaces, or **margins**, on the top, bottom, left, and right of your writing.

- Leave more space between sentences than between words.

Not OK

The Moon and the Earth

The Moon is very different from the Earth. Unlike the Earth the Moon does not have air or water. Nothing lives on the Moon.

Present It!

OK

The first sentence is **indented**.

The writing begins at the **left margin**.

The writing leaves space for the **right margin**.

The Moon and the Earth

The Moon is very different from the Earth. Unlike the Earth the Moon does not have air or water. Nothing lives on the Moon.

Present It!

Spell Sounds in English

Say the word you want to spell.
Write the letters that spell the sounds.

Spell Consonant Sounds

b

ball

ca**b**

c

cat

d

desk

re**d**

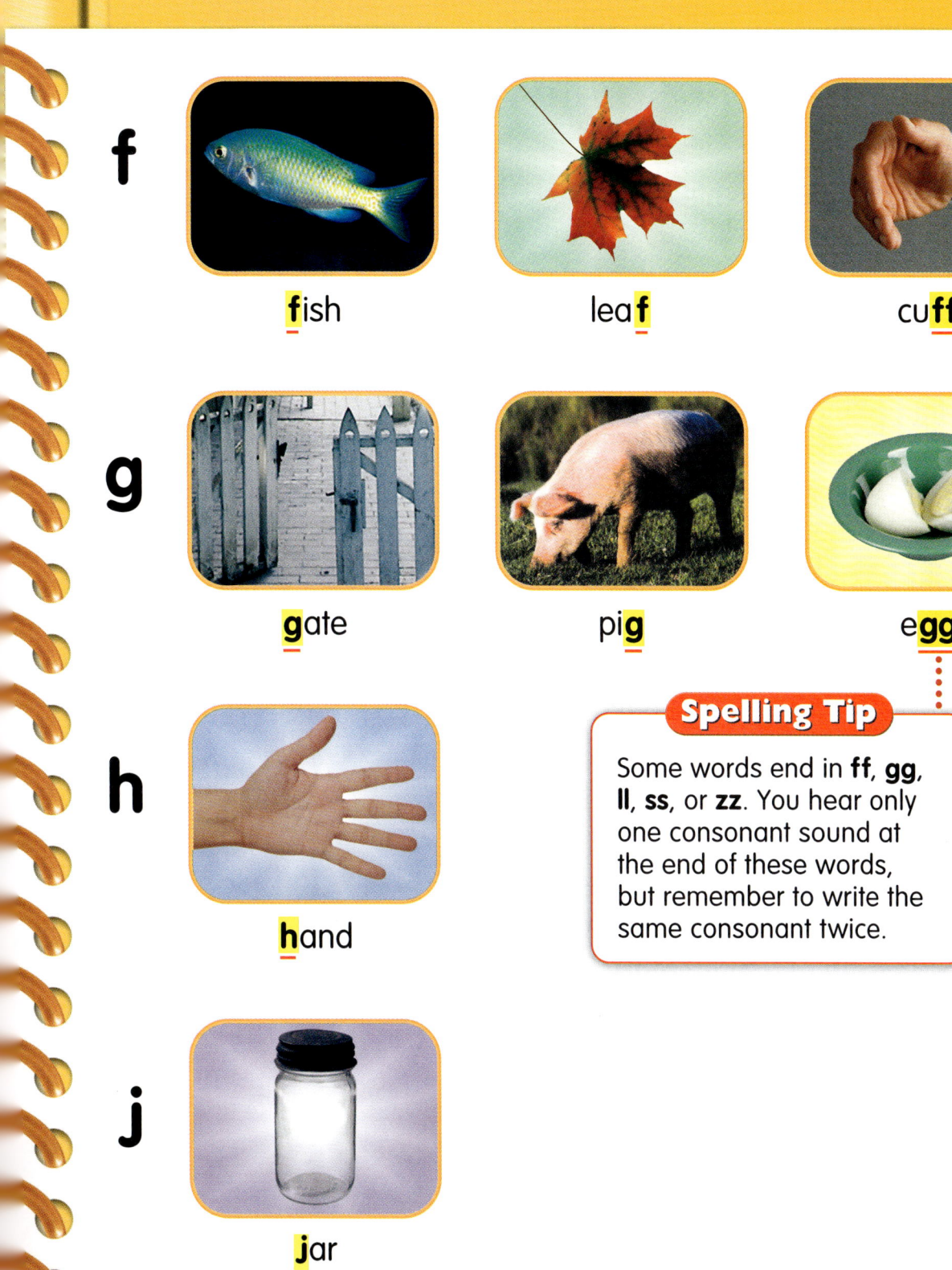

f

fish leaf cuff

g

gate pig egg

Spelling Tip

Some words end in **ff**, **gg**, **ll**, **ss**, or **zz**. You hear only one consonant sound at the end of these words, but remember to write the same consonant twice.

h

hand

j

jar

Present It!

Spell Consonant Sounds, continued

k

key

bea**k**

ba**ck**

Spelling Tip
Key and **cat** begin with the same sound. Spell the sound with **k** when the letter **e** or **i** comes next.

Spelling Tip
If the vowel is short, like the **a** in **back**, you usually write **c** before **k**.

l

lamp

hee**l**

be**ll**

m

map

dru**m**

Present It!

Spell Consonant Sounds, continued

r

red

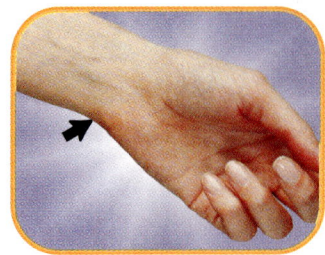
wrist

Spelling Tip
Some words have a silent **w** before **r**. Can you think of another word? Here's a clue: wr

s

seed

ki**ss**

t

ten

ha**t**

mi**tt**

v

van

Spelling Tip
Words never end in **v**. Write **ve** at the end of words like **have** and **give**.

Present It!

w

wagon

x

si**x**

y

yellow

z

zero   fi**zz**

Present It!

Spell Short Vowel Sounds

short **a**

apple

m**a**n

short **e**

egg

j**e**t

short **i**

inch

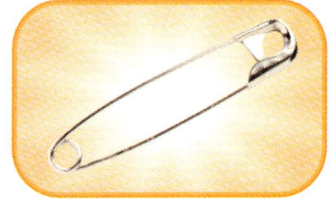
p**i**n

short **o**

ox

p**o**t

short **u**

up

b**u**s

Present It!

Spell One Sound with Two Letters

shell

fi**sh**

whale

thumb

ba**th**

ri**ng**

chin

pea**ch**

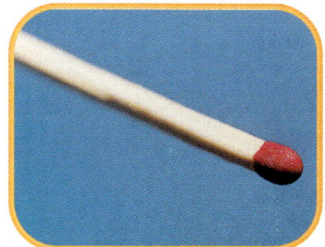
ma**tch**

Spelling Tip

If the vowel is short, like the **a** in **match**, you usually write **t** before **ch**.

Present It!

Spell Two Sounds with Two Letters

gi**ft**

o**ld** be**lt**

la**mp**

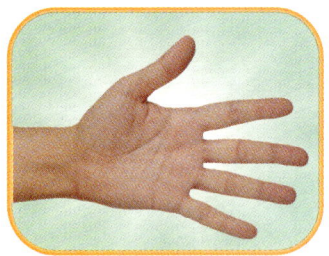
ha**nd**

ba**nk**

a**nt**

di**sk**

ne**st**

Present It!

truck

brush

green

frog

drum

crow

clock

plant

flag

smell

snap

stamp

Present It! 213

Spell Long Vowels

long **a**

c**ake**

s**ai**l

gr**ay**

long **e**

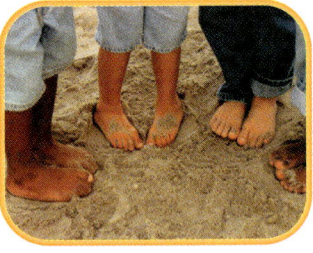
f**ee**t

s**ea**

bunn**y**

long **i**

k**i**t**e**

t**ie**

n**igh**t

sk**y**

Present It!

long o

r**o**pe

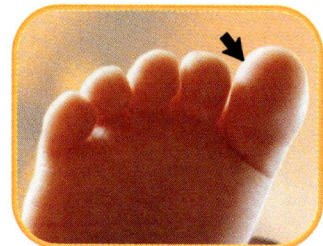
cr**ow**

b**oa**t

t**oe**

long u

t**u**be

bl**ue**

fr**ui**t

Spelling Tip

Some very short words end with a long vowel sound. Just write one letter for the long vowel sound in these words:

be	he	me	go	no
she	hi	we	so	

Present It!

Spell Words with *c* and *g*

hard c

cat

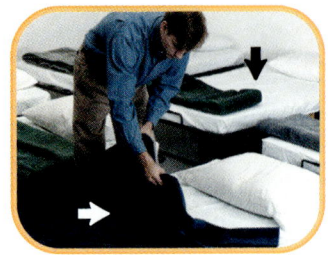
cot

cup

soft c

city

cent

rice

hard g

gate

go

gum

soft g

ginger

gem

Spelling Tip

Use **ge** in words like **age** and **huge** that have a long vowel. Use **dge** in words like **bridge** and **edge** that have a short vowel.

Present It!

Spell Words with Vowel + *r*

st**ar**

h**or**n

f**er**n

t**ur**n

b**ir**d

ch**air**

b**ear**

Spelling Tip

Say the word you want to spell. Listen for the **r**. Does **r** come after the vowel like **bird**, or before the vowel like **brick**?

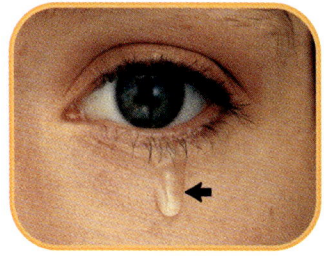
t**ear**

d**eer**

Present It! 217

Spell More Vowel Sounds

c**oi**n

b**oy**

> **Spelling Tip**
>
> The letters **oi** and **oy** spell the same sound. Use **oy** if you hear the sound at the end of a word.

cl**ou**d

cr**ow**n

> **Spelling Tip**
>
> The letters **ou** and **ow** spell the same sound. Use **ow** if you hear the sound at the end of a word like **now**.

m**oo**n

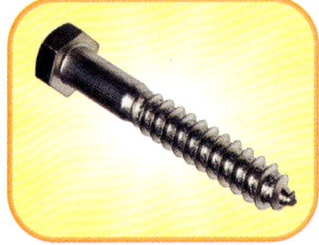

scr**ew**

Present It!

l**au**nch

s**aw**

s**al**t

b**all**

Spelling Tip

If you can spell **ball**, you can spell **call**, **fall**, **tall**, **small**, and **wall**.

b**oo**k

Spelling Tip

If you can spell **book**, you can spell **brook**, **cook**, **hook**, **look**, and **took**.

Spell Words with -ed, -ing, -er, -est

■ Just add the ending to words like **lift** and **rain**.

Examples: lift + ed = lift**ed**   rain + ing = rain**ing**

1 vowel + 2 consonants

2 vowels + 1 consonant

■ When a word ends in silent **e**, drop the **e**. Then add the ending.

Examples: hop~~e~~ + ed = hop**ed**

rid~~e~~ + ing = rid**ing**

nic~~e~~ + er = nic**er**

nic~~e~~ + est = nic**est**

larg**e**

larg **er**

Present It!

■ When a word ends in one vowel and one consonant, double the consonant. Then add the ending.

    Examples: hop + p + ed = hopp**ed**

                   skip + p + ing = skipp**ing**

                   big + g + er = bigg**er**

                   big + g + est = bigg**est**

■ When a word ends in a consonant and **y**, change **y** to **i**. Then add -**ed**, -**er**, or -**est**.

    Examples: study + ed = studi**ed**

                   happy + er = happi**er**

                   happy + est = happi**est**

■ Keep the **y** when you add -**ing**

    Examples: fly + ing = fly**ing**

                   try + ing = try**ing**

                   study + ing = study**ing**

Present It!

Spell Plurals

■ Add -**s** to most words.

Examples:

pot + s = pot**s**   kite + s = kite**s**

■ Add -**es** to words that end in **s**, **ch**, **sh**, **x**, or **z**.

Examples:

glass + es = glass**es**   peach + es = peach**es**

brush + es = brush**es**   box + es = box**es**

■ Change **y** to **i**. Add -**es**.

Examples:

baby + es = babi**es**   puppy + es = puppi**es**

Present It!

Spell Long Words

- Say the word and count the parts. Spell each part. Then read the word.

    Example: bas + ket = basket

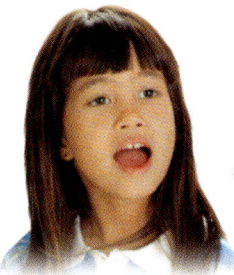

> The word is **basket**. I hear two parts. I'll write the first part: **bas**. Then I'll write the second part: **ket**.

- Is the long word made up of two smaller words? Write each word.

    Example: week + end = weekend

- Does the word have the first sound in **about**? Start with **a**.

    Examples: **a**long **a**cross **a**round **a**lone

- Does the word end like **apple**? Many words end in a **consonant** + **le**.

    Examples: can**dle** lit**tle** ta**ble** ti**tle**

> **Spelling Tip**
>
> If the word has a long vowel sound like **table** and **title**, write only one consonant before **le**.

Present It!

Spell These Right!

Some words are hard to spell. You can look here to check your spelling.

Words That Sound Alike

its
it's

Its fur is dirty.

It's time for a bath.

> **Spelling Tip**
>
> Say the sentence. Does "it is" make sense? If so, use **it's**.

knew
new

She **knew** the answer.

She has a **new** pencil.

> **Spelling Tip**
>
> Think about the word's meaning. **New** means the opposite of **old**.

know
no

Do you **know** how to dance?

No, I can't dance.

our
hour

Our bus is late!

It will be here in one **hour**.

Present It!

they're
there
their

They're playing on the swings.

There is a bee on **their** dad!

through
threw

She walked **through** the gate.

He **threw** her a ball.

two
to
too

Two friends are going **to** the movies.

Can we go, **too**?

wear
where

I want to **wear** my red jacket.

Where is it?

your
you're

Spelling Tip

Say the sentence. Does "you are" make sense? If so, use **you're**.

Your book report is great!

You're learning to spell.

Words That Kids Misspell

above
The clock is **above** the door.

again
Let's sing this song **again**.

almost
I can **almost** reach the shelf.

always
She **always** uses a blue pen.

another
I need **another** piece of paper.

anyone
Does **anyone** want more cake?

are
You **are** in the wrong seat!

beautiful
Your new dress is **beautiful**.

because
He can't play **because** he is sick.

before
I wash my hands **before** I eat.

could
You **could** be an astronaut.

country
Mexico is a **country**.

different
We are on two **different** teams.

enough
There is **enough** cake for ten.

especially
I **especially** liked the panda.

everything
Everything is ready for the party.

except
I like all fruit, **except** for peaches.

excited
She's **excited** about her new toy.

favorite
Blue is my **favorite** color.

first
This is the **first** time I tried to skate.

friends
She likes to play with her **friends**.

getting
He is **getting** good grades now.

Present It!

into
They jumped **into** the pool.

laugh
I like to **laugh** at your jokes.

myself
I baked this bread by **myself**!

people
The city is full of **people**.

really
We **really** miss you!

said
They **said**, "Hi!"

school
I take the bus to **school**.

something
They forgot **something**.

sometimes
Sometimes Jill is late for school.

terrible
Last night there was a **terrible** storm.

thought
I **thought** I saw a bear!

trouble
We had **trouble** lifting the heavy boxes.

until
Wait **until** the light turns green.

usually
I **usually** study in my room.

very
You did a **very** good job!

want
Do you **want** an apple?

were
They **were** in the same class last year.

who
Who is your teacher?

Present It!

Spelling Tips

Here are some tips to help you spell words correctly.

1. **Look** at the new word.

2. **Look again** and **say** the word.

3. **Listen** to the word as you **say it again**.

4. **Make a picture** of the word in your head.

5. Spell the word out loud several times.

6. Write the word five or ten times.

7. Check the word. Look in a dictionary.

8. Use the word in a sentence.

Use a Dictionary

Use a dictionary to find out the meaning or spelling of a word. All dictionaries list the words in **alphabetical order**, or from A to Z.

Picture Dictionary

A **picture dictionary** uses mainly pictures and examples to show the meaning of a word.

Look at the **first letter** of your word. To look up the word **idea**, turn to the page that shows the letter **i**.

The **second letter** of each word is in **alphabetical order**, too. The word **idea** comes after **ice** because **d** comes after **c**.

Examples and pictures help you understand what a word means.

230 **Present It!**

Beginning Dictionary

A **beginning dictionary** uses simple words to explain the meaning of a word. Sometimes a beginning dictionary also gives examples and pictures.

These words are **guide words**. They show the first and last words on the page. Use the guide words to help you find your word.

fountain / fresh

Alexander was hot and thirsty and was happy to find this **fountain**.

fountain
A **fountain** is a stream of water that shoots up into the air. Some **fountains** are pretty to look at. Other **fountains** are used for drinking.
▲ **fountains**.

Fourth of July
The **Fourth of July** is an American holiday that celebrates the birthday of the United States. It is also called **Independence Day**.

fox
A **fox** is a wild animal. Most **foxes** look like small, thin dogs, but they have thick fur and a big tail. They also have large ears that are pointed and a long nose. ▲ **foxes**.

free
1. **Free** means that a person does not have to pay any money for something. The magic show in the park is **free**. There is a **free** toy in every box of that cereal.
2. **Free** also means not held back or kept in. The cat was **free** to walk around.
▲ **freer, freest**.

freeze
Freeze means to become solid when it is very cold. When water **freezes**, it changes into ice. We skated on the pond after it **froze**.
▲ **froze, frozen, freezing**.

fresh
1. When something is **fresh**, it has just been made, done, or gathered. We ate **fresh** tomatoes from June's garden. Our supermarket sells **fresh** fish. This bread was baked this morning and is very **fresh**.
2. **Fresh** also means not having salt. Water in rivers, lakes, and ponds is **fresh** water. Water in the ocean is salt water. ▲ **fresher, freshest**.

136

A **definition** uses simple words to explain the meaning of a word.

Sometimes a word has more than one meaning.

Examples help you understand what a word means and how to use it.

Present It! 231

Sometimes English is like a puzzle. How do you put the pieces together? You can learn the rules of grammar.

Lisa helps Marcus.
She helps Marcus.

Sentences

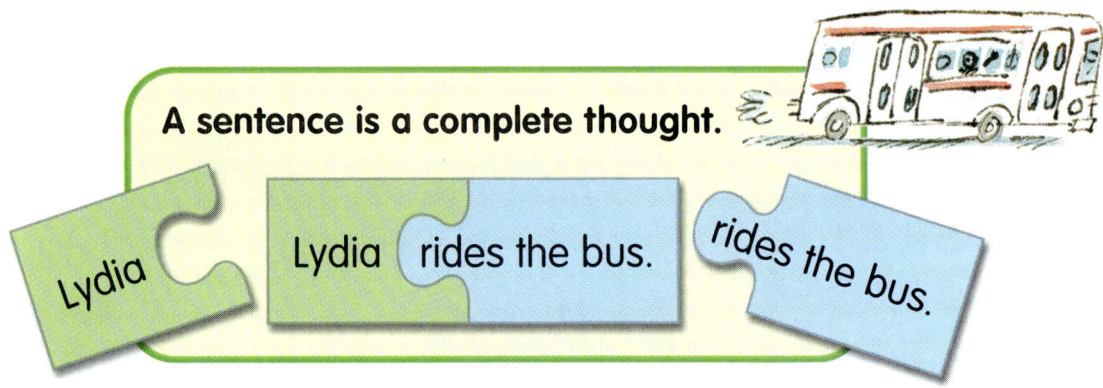

A sentence is a complete thought.

Lydia Lydia rides the bus. rides the bus.

All sentences start with a **capital letter**.

Example: **M**any people work in the city.

There are four kinds of sentences.

❶ Statements

A statement tells something. It ends with a **period**.

Examples: People walk to their jobs.
A policeman stops the traffic. **period**

234 Grammar Made Graphic

❷ Questions

A question asks for information. It ends with a **question mark**.

There are many ways to start a question.

Examples:

Are the hot dogs good?
How much is a hot dog?
Is there some mustard?
Where are the buns?
Who wants pickles?

Which balloons are for sale?
Do you want the big balloon?
Does it have a string?
Can the big balloon fly high?
When can I take it?

question mark

Grammar Made Graphic

3 Exclamations

A sentence that shows strong feeling is called an **exclamation**. It ends with an **exclamation point**.

Examples: Wow, the buildings are so tall! ← **exclamation point**
That car is going too fast!

4 Commands

A **command** tells you to do something. Many commands end with a **period**. If a command shows strong feeling, it ends with an **exclamation point**.

Examples: Stop at the corner.
Please look both ways before you cross the street. ← **period**
Watch out for that car!
                        ↑
             exclamation point

Go To ▶ Practice A on page 322.

Negative Sentences

> A negative sentence uses a **negative word** like **not** or **never**.
>
>
>
> **Example:** She is happy.   She is **not** happy.

In a negative sentence, the word **not** comes after **am**, **is**, or **are**.

Examples:

I **am** **not** a good swimmer.

The water **is** **not** warm.

I am afraid of the water, but the other kids **are** **not** afraid.

They **are** **never** tired of the water!

Use only one negative word in a sentence.

Our pool is ~~not~~ never closed.

Go To Practice B on page 322.

Grammar Made Graphic

Complete Sentences

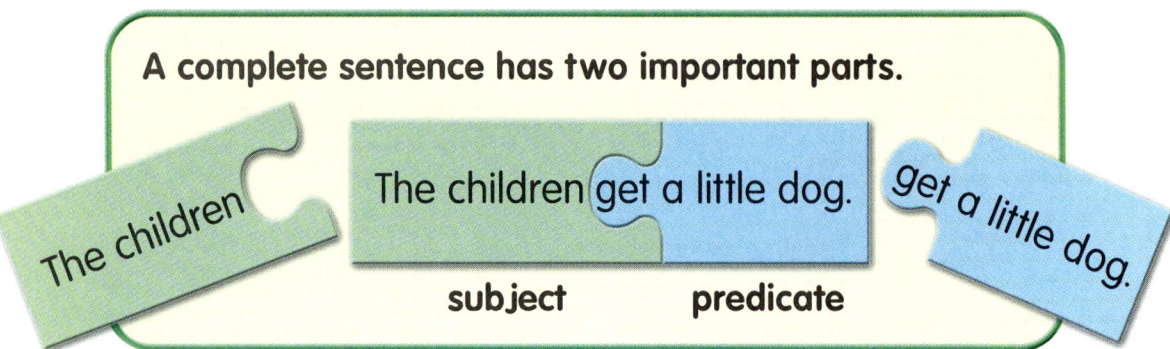

A complete sentence has two important parts.

The children | The children get a little dog. | get a little dog.
subject — predicate

■ Every sentence has two parts.

The **subject** tells whom or what the sentence is about.

Mom is tired.
She sits on the bench.
The children play with their dog.
The brown dog has a stick.
The stick is long.

The **predicate** tells what the subject is, does, or has.

Longer Sentences

You can use <u>and</u> or <u>or</u> to combine two short sentences into a longer sentence.

Example: Juan goes to the pool.
Tina goes to the pool.
Juan **and** Tina go to the pool.

■ You can combine the **subjects** of two sentences.

Examples:

1. **Juan** likes the pool.
   Tina likes the pool.
   Juan and Tina like the pool.

2. **Juan's dad** takes them.
   Tina's mom takes them.
   Juan's dad or Tina's mom takes them.

■ You can combine the **predicates** of two sentences.

Examples:

3. Juan **likes to dive**.
   Juan **likes to splash**.
   Juan **likes to dive and splash**.

4. Tina **swims**.
   Tina **goes down the slide**.
   Tina **swims or goes down the slide**.

Grammar Made Graphic

Longer Sentences, continued

■ You can also combine two sentences into a compound sentence. Use **and**, **but**, or **or**.

and	Use **and** to put together two ideas that are alike. + Tina went to the pool. Then she went shopping. Tina went to the pool**,** **and** then she went shopping.
but	Use **but** to put together two ideas that show a difference. + Juan had fun on the slide. He did not like the diving board. Juan had fun on the slide**,** **but** he did not like the diving board.
or	Use **or** to show a choice between two ideas. + Tina can swim after school. She can do her homework. Tina can swim after school**,** **or** she can do her homework.

Grammar Tip

When you connect two sentences with **and**, **but**, or **or**, you make a **compound sentence**. You use a **comma** in a compound sentence.

Practices E and F on page 324.

Write Sentences

When you write, use different kinds of sentences. They make your writing interesting.

Example: Pam looks up at the building. How tall is it? Wow! The top reaches the clouds!

Pam looks at the wide city street. It is full of cars and buses. The traffic does not move. ^(What is wrong? Oh, now she can see!) Too many people are crossing the street. Many cars ~~honk their horns.~~ ^(and) Many trucks honk their horns. ^(They are loud!)

The writer added different kinds of sentences, and she combined two sentences at the end. Now the writing is more interesting.

Grammar Made Graphic 241

Common Nouns

Some words name people, animals, places, or things. These naming words are called nouns.

Examples:

Person	Animal	Place	Thing
girl	dog	park	bench

The girl takes her dog to the park. They sit on a bench.

■ Some **nouns** name **people** or **animals**.

Examples: The girl and her mother feed a duck.
The dog chases a bird.

Can you name other **people** and **animals** in the picture?

Grammar Made Graphic

- Some **nouns** name **things**.

    Examples: When it's time to eat, they find a **table**.
    It is near a pretty **flower**.
    The girl and her mom eat a **sandwich**.
    The dog eats out of his **bowl**.

Can you name other **things** in the picture?

Grammar Made Graphic

Common Nouns, continued

■ Some **nouns** name **places**.

Examples: The girl and her mom leave the **park**.
They walk along the **street**.
They pass by the **museum**.
They stop and look in a **store**.

Can you name other **places** in the picture?

Proper Nouns

A **proper noun** is the name of a special person, animal, place, or thing. Start a proper noun with a capital letter.

Example:

I see a boy with a cat.   Oh, it's **Bill** with his cat **Fluffy**!

Which nouns name special people and animals?

People and Animals	
girl	Lynn
boy	Bill
cat	Fluffy

Which nouns name special places?

Places	
store	Books and More
street	West Street
park	Chávez Park

Which nouns start with a capital letter?

 Practice A on page 325.

Grammar Made Graphic

More than One

> A **singular noun** names one person, animal, place, or thing. A **plural noun** names more than one.
>
> **Example:** You can buy one **book** or many **books** at the store.

■ Add **-s** to most nouns to show more than one.

■ Add **-es** to nouns that end in **s**, **ss**, **x**, **ch**, **sh**, and **z**.

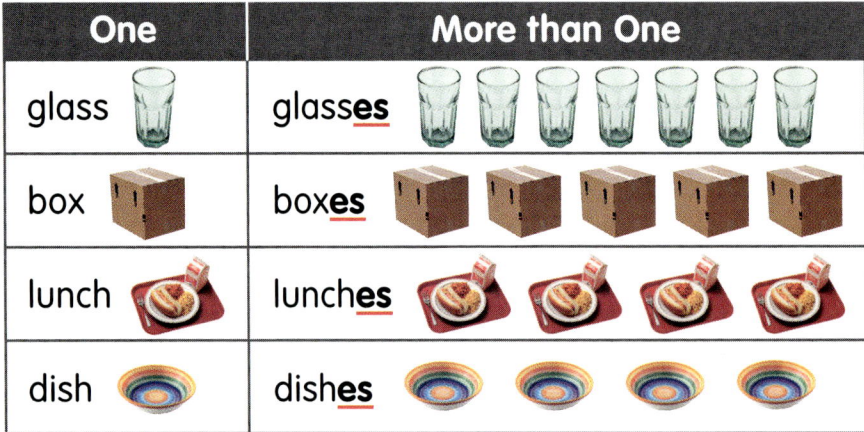

Grammar Made Graphic

■ For nouns that end in **-y**, change the **y** to **i** and then add **-es**.

One	More than One
cherry	cher**ries**
berry	ber**ries**
baby	bab**ies**

■ A few nouns change in special ways to show more than one.

One	More than One
man	men
woman	women
child	children
foot	feet

Go To ▶ Practice B on page 325.

Grammar Made Graphic 247

A, An, and The

> The words **a**, **an**, and **the** often come just before a noun.
>
> **Example:** You can get **a hat** and **an apple** at **the carnival**.

■ Use **a** or **an** when you are not thinking of something specific.

Examples: Efram plans to go to **an event** this year.

He wants to play **a game**.

He wants to get **a bag** of popcorn.

CITY EVENTS
May 7 — Spring Carnival at Adams School
July 4 — Fourth of July Picnic in Chávez Park
October 7 — Fall Festival at Central Square
December 12 — Winter Wonderland at Harding Mall

■ Use **a** if the next word starts with a **consonant**.

Examples: a **f**estival
a **c**arnival
a **g**ame

■ Use **an** if the next word starts with a **vowel or silent h**.

Examples: an **a**nimal
an **e**vent
an **i**dea
an **o**rchestra
an **u**mbrella
an **h**our

Grammar Made Graphic

■ Use **the** when you are thinking of something specific.

Examples: Efram goes to **the Spring Carnival**.
He watches **the puppets**.
He likes **the popcorn** that his father bought.

Go To Practice C on page 326.

Grammar Made Graphic

Possessive Nouns

A **possessive noun** is the name of an owner. The name always has an apostrophe (').

Examples: **Mike's** trucks are very big.
The **trucks'** noise is very loud!

Study these examples to learn where to write the apostrophe.

- For one owner, add the apostrophe **'** plus **s**.

- For more than one owner, just add the apostrophe **'**.

One Owner	More than One Owner
the **car's** horn	the **cars'** horns
the **worker's** hammer	the **workers'** hammers

The **car's** horn wakes me up in the morning.

I know! The **trucks'** engines are really loud, too!

Use Nouns in Writing

Use **precise nouns** to help your reader know just what you are writing about.

Example: A **car** parks outside the **office**.
A **taxi** parks outside the **clinic**.

The writer changed the words **sound** and **noise** to be specific.

City Noises

I do not need an alarm. The city noises wake me up. I hear the sound [toot] of a taxi rushing along the street. I hear the noise [clang and bang] of trash cans in the alley. I hear the wail of a car [an ambulance]. Toot, clang, wail! It is time to get up!

The word **car** is good, but **ambulance** is even more precise!

Go To ▶ Practice E on page 326.

Grammar Made Graphic 251

Pronouns

> A **pronoun** can take the place of a noun.
>
> Example: **Clare** writes a letter.
>
> **She** writes a letter.

You can use these pronouns in the subject of a sentence. Be sure to use the pronoun that tells about the right number of people.

- Use **I** for yourself.
- Use **we** for yourself and another person.

One	More than One
I	we
you	you
he, she, it	they

I finished my letter.

We will take it to the post office.

I want to go, too. Can **we** take Boomer?

Grammar Tip

Always capitalize the pronoun **I**, wherever it appears in a sentence.

Grammar Made Graphic

- Use **you** when you talk to one person or to more than one person.

Pronouns, continued

■ When you talk about one other person:

- Use **he** for a boy or a man.
- Use **she** for a girl or a woman.

■ When you talk about more than one person, use **they**.

Grammar Made Graphic

Pronouns, continued

■ When you talk about places and things:

- Use **it** for one place or thing.
- Use **they** for more than one place or thing.

Some pronouns tell who owns something.

Example: This is **Clare's** letter.

This is **her** letter.

■ Use the pronoun that tells about the right person or people.

Pronouns, continued

> **Remember:** A **pronoun** can take the place of a noun.
>
> **Examples:** Mrs. Ramos needs **posters**.
>
> Mrs. Ramos needs **them**.
>
> Clare will make some for **Mrs. Ramos**.
>
> Clare will make some for **her**.

■ Use these pronouns after action verbs or after words like **to**, **for**, **at**, **of**, or **with**.

One	More than One
me	us
you	you
him, her, it	them

- Use **me** for yourself.
- Use **us** for yourself and another person.
- Use **you** to talk to other people.

258 Grammar Made Graphic

- Use **him** for one boy or one man.
- Use **her** for one girl or one woman.
- Use **it** for one place or thing.
- Use **them** for more than one person, place, or thing.

Give this marker to **him**. They can use **it** to make the posters.

Clare will make the posters. I will help **her**.

When you finish the posters, I will hang **them** in the neighborhood.

This, That, These, Those

Use **this** or **these** to talk about things that are near you.

Use **that** or **those** to talk about things that are far from you.

	One	More than One
Near	this	these
Far	that	those

Use Pronouns in Writing

When you repeat the same noun too often, your writing is not very interesting. Change some nouns to pronouns. Make sure you use the correct pronoun!

Example: My friend and I picked up trash at the park.
~~My friend and I~~ **We** put ~~the trash~~ **it** in plastic bags.

The use of pronouns makes the paragraph sound better.

Why did the writer change **his** to **her**?

Neighborhood Clean-Up

Neighbors cleaned up the park on Saturday. Mr. Carter painted a bench. ~~Mr. Carter~~ **He** did a good job! ~~Mr. Carter's~~ **His** children, Ray and Clare, picked up leaves. ~~Ray and Clare~~ **They** filled up two bags.

Mrs. Sánchez and ~~his~~ **her** son worked hard, too. Their job was to plant flowers. Mr. and Mrs. Ross trimmed the bushes.

The park looks great now!

Grammar Made Graphic 261

Adjectives

> An **adjective** describes, or tells about, a noun.
>
> Example: The car went up a hill.
>
> The **red** car went up a **little** hill.

■ Many adjectives tell how something looks. They tell about **size**, **color**, and **shape**. How does this bus look?

size
The **big** bus takes children to school.

color
The **yellow** bus has **red** lights.

shape
The wheels on the bus are **round**.

Practice A on page 330.

■ Some adjectives tell "how many" or "how much".

Use **number words** to tell exactly how many things there are.

Examples: The train has **six** cars.
It has **one** engine.
The train will travel **120** miles to Houston.

Sometimes, you do not know the exact number. Then use the words in the chart.

More Ways to Tell "How Many" or "How Much"

Use these words when it is possible to count things.	Use these words when it is not possible to count things.
a lot of cars **many** cars **several** cars	**much** rain **a lot of** rain
some cars **a few** cars	**a little** rain **some** rain **not much** rain **only a little** rain

Go To ▶ Practice B on page 330.

Grammar Made Graphic

Adjectives That Compare

> **Adjectives** can help you compare things.
>
> "Compare" means to show how things are alike or different.
>
> **Example:** This is a **small** car.
> This car is **smaller** than that one.
> This is the **smallest** car of all.

■ Add **-er** to an adjective to compare two things. You will probably use the word **than** in your sentence, too.

Examples: The van is **taller than** the car.
The truck is **cleaner than** the van.

■ Add **-est** to an adjective to compare three or more things. Use the word **the** before the adjective.

Examples: The truck is **the tallest** of the three.
The car is **the cleanest** of all.

Grammar Made Graphic

Go To ▶ Practice C on page 331.

■ Do not add **-er** or **-est** to a long adjective. Adjectives with three or more syllables would be hard to say with **-er** or **-est** at the end. Use **more** or **most** with long adjectives.

Examples:

The blue car is **expensive**.
The black van is **more expensive** than the blue car.
The red car is **the most expensive** car of all.

■ Some adjectives have special forms for comparing things.

This taxi looks **bad**.   This taxi looks **worse**.   This taxi looks the **worst** of all!

This bus looks **good**.   This bus looks **better**.   This bus looks the **best** of all!

Adjectives in Sentences

You can use **adjectives** in the subject or predicate of a sentence.

Examples:

The **green** car stops here.
subject — predicate

Its seats are **green**, too.
subject — predicate

- Most adjectives come before the nouns they tell about.

    Examples: The **green** car is on a **wide** street.

    The **little** truck has a **loud** motor.

- An adjective can come after words like **is**, **are**, **look**, **feel**, **smell**, and **taste**. The adjective tells about the noun in the subject.

    Examples: Dad is **careful**.

    Kazuo feels **safe**.

Grammar Made Graphic

Use Adjectives in Writing

> When you write, use **adjectives**. They help your reader see what you are writing about.
>
> **Example:** The plane left the airport.
> The **silver** plane left the **huge** airport.

Now you know how many houses and roads the writer saw.

My Trip on an Airplane

I went on a big, silver plane. It flew high in the sky. I saw _^houses *(two)* and _^roads *(many)* below. There were _^cows *(tiny)* and horses, too. Then we went up even higher. I saw _^clouds *(fluffy)*. They looked like white pillows, and I fell asleep. When we landed with a bump, I woke up. It was a great trip!

This **adjective** helps you picture the clouds.

Go To Practice E on page 332.

Grammar Made Graphic 267

The Verbs *Am*, *Is*, and *Are*

> Some verbs do not show action. These **verbs** tell what the subject of a sentence is or is like.
>
> **Examples:** Mr. Silva **is** the coach.
> He **is** happy.

■ Be sure to use the verb that goes with the subject.

1. Use **am** with **I**.
2. Use **is** with **he**, **she**, or **it**.

Hi! **I am** Mr. Silva.

He is the best coach!

3. Use **are** with **you**, **we**, or **they**.

Are they on Coach Silva's team, too?

Yes, **they are**.

We are all on Coach Silva's team! **Are you** on a team?

The Verbs *Has* and *Have*

> **Some verbs tell what the subject of a sentence has.**
>
> **Examples:** This team **has** good players.
> We **have** a difficult game.

■ Be sure to use the verb that goes with the subject.

1. Use **have** with **I**   **2.** Use **has** with **he**, **she**, or **it**.

"I **have** a good idea for a play!"

"He always **has** good ideas!"

3. Use **have** with **you**, **we**, or **they**.

"We **have** the ball. You **have** a chance to score."

"Oh, no! They **have** a great goalie!"

Go To ▶ Practice B on page 333.

Grammar Made Graphic

Actions in the Present

All action verbs show when the action happens.

Example: I **kick** the ball.

This **verb** is in the **present tense**.
The action is happening **now**.

■ Use **s** at the end of an action verb if the subject is **he**, **she**, or **it**.

He	The player **kicks** the ball. Tim **kicks** the ball. He **kicks** the ball.
She	The girl **kicks** the ball. Maritza **kicks** the ball. She **kicks** the ball.
It	The ball **rolls** into the goal. It **rolls** into the goal.

■ Do not use **s** for **I**, **you**, **we**, or **they**.

Examples: I **kick** the ball.
We **kick** the ball.
You **kick** the ball.
They **kick** the ball.

Practices C and D on pages 334–33

Grammar Made Graphic

Actions in the Past

You can add **-ed** to many action verbs to show that the action happened **in the past**.

Example: I **kicked** the ball.

This **verb** is in the **past tense**.

Compare the verbs in the chart.

	Now	In the Past
1.	We **play** a good game.	We **played** a good game yesterday.
2.	My friends **pass** me the ball.	My friends **passed** me the ball.
3.	I **kick** a goal!	I **kicked** a goal!
4.	I **yell**, "GOAL!"	I **yelled**, "GOAL!"
5.	My friends **cheer** for me.	My friends **cheered** for me.
6.	My mom and dad **kiss** me!	My mom and dad **kissed** me!

Go To Practices E and F on page 336.

Grammar Made Graphic

More Actions in the Past

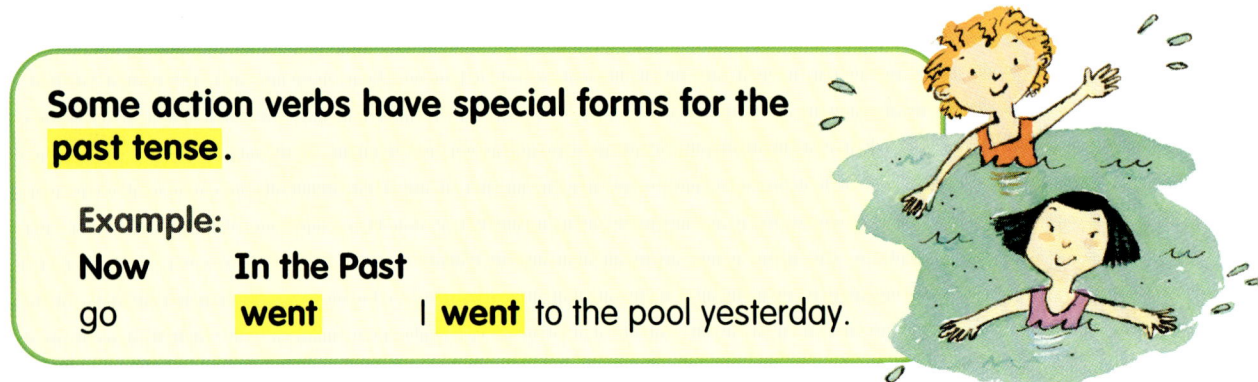

Some action verbs have special forms for the **past tense**.

Example:
Now	In the Past	
go	**went**	I **went** to the pool yesterday.

Compare the verbs in the chart.

	Now	In the Past
1.	I **bring** my friend Tina to the pool.	I **brought** my friend Tina to the pool.
2.	We **do** some stretches.	We **did** some stretches.
3.	We **get** ready to swim.	We **got** ready to swim.
4.	We **go** in the water.	We **went** in the water.
5.	I **give** Tina a lesson.	I **gave** Tina a lesson.
6.	She **holds** her breath.	She **held** her breath.
7.	She **makes** it across the pool.	She **made** it across the pool.
8.	Her mom **sees** her on the other side.	Her mom **saw** her on the other side.
9.	"Good job, Tina," she **says**.	"Good job, Tina," she **said**.
10.	Tina **takes** another swim, and I **take** a rest!	Tina **took** another swim, and I **took** a rest!

Grammar Made Graphic

Go To ▶ Practice G on page 337.

The verbs **was** and **were** tell about something that happened **in the past**.

Examples:
Now   In the Past
am   **was**   I **was** a good teacher.
are   **were**   Tina and I **were** in a race.

Study this chart.

Now	In the Past
I **am**	I **was**
you **are**	you **were**
he, she, it **is**	he, she, it **was**
we **are**	we **were**
they **are**	they **were**

■ Use **was** and **were** to tell about the past.

- Use **was** with **I**.

    Example: I **was** very surprised.

- Use **was** with **he**, **she**, or **it**.

    Example: She **was** very fast!

- Use **were** with **you**, **we**, or **they**.

    Example: We won the race.
    We **were** so happy!

Practice H on page 338.

Grammar Made Graphic

Actions in the Future

> **Some verbs tell what will happen later.**
>
> Example: I **will visit** you next winter.
>
> I **am going to play** in the snow.
>
> These **verbs** are in the **future tense**.

■ There are two ways to make a verb tell about the future.

- You can add **will** before the verb.
- You can write **am going to**, **are going to**, or **is going to** before the verb.

Next winter, we **will have** snow.

We **are going to make** a snowman.

María **is going to ride** on her sled.

Ahmed **will skate**.

276   Grammar Made Graphic

Helping Verbs

A **helping verb** works with another verb. The other verb is called the main verb.

Examples: We **are** playing basketball.
We **can** play well!

Together, the helping verb and the main verb tell about an action.

■ Some verbs tell about an action as it is happening.

- These verbs use **am**, **is**, or **are** as the **helping verb**.
- They use **-ing** at the end of the **main verb**.

I **am** running fast.

He **is** bouncing the ball.

She **is** reaching for the ball.

They **are** watching.

Grammar Made Graphic

■ Some **helping verbs** have special meanings.

- Use **can** to tell that someone is able to do an action.

    Example:

    I **can bounce** the ball!

- Use **may** and **might** to tell that something is possible.

    Examples:

    We **may play** again later.
    Our team **might win**.

- Use **must** and **should** to tell that somebody has to do something.

    Examples:

    We **must practice** more.
    I **should pass** the ball better.

Grammar Made Graphic

Helping Verbs, continued

■ You can use a **helping verb** to start a question. The subject comes between the **helping verb** and the **main verb**.

   Examples: **Do** you **like** this game?

   Does Dad **play** this game?

   Is Mom **watching** us?

   Are they **looking** now?

   Can you **throw** the ball to me?

■ In a negative sentence, put **not** between the **helping verb** and the **main verb**.

Does he catch it?
No, he **does not catch** it.

Go To ▶ Practice J on page 339.

Use Verbs in Writing

> **Vivid verbs** make your writing more interesting. They give your reader a good picture of the action.
>
> **Example:** We **went** up to the ice and **skated** in.
> We **rushed** up to the ice and **glided** in.

Can you see what the skater is doing? The **vivid verbs** help you see.

Ice Skating

Higher and higher
I **glide** in the sky,
My feet flashing silver,
A star in each eye.
With wind at my back
I can **float**, I can **soar**.
The earth cannot hold me
In place anymore.

—Sandra Liatsos

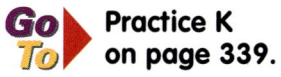

Grammar Made Graphic 281

Adverbs

> An **adverb** can tell more about a **verb**.
>
> Example: Josh **sleeps** in his room.
> Josh **sleeps** **quietly** in his room.

- Many adverbs tell **how** something happens. These **adverbs** often end in **-ly**.

    Examples: Josh **gets up** **quickly**.

    Josh and Aunt Sue **walk** **fast** to the train station.

- Some adverbs tell **where** something happens.

    Examples: The subway **stops** **there**.

    Josh and Aunt Sue **will travel** **north** on the train.

- Some adverbs tell **when** something happens.

    Examples: On Saturdays, they **always** **go** to the Science Center.

    They **will arrive** **soon**.

Use Adverbs in Writing

Use **adverbs** to tell where, when, and how things happen. These details help make your writing clear and interesting.

Example: Josh and Aunt Sue looked **carefully** at the exhibit in the Science Center.

Josh added adverbs to give important details.

The adverb **loudly** tells Grandma just how the dinosaur roared.

> 256 South Vista Drive
> Silver City, Arizona
> May 4, 2003
>
> Dear Grandma,
>
> *Yesterday* I went with Aunt Sue to the Science Center. We go there every Saturday. There was a special dinosaur exhibit. Big robots showed how dinosaurs moved!
>
> You can control the robots with levers, just like a video game. When you press a button, the dinosaurs roar *loudly*. It was a little scary. It was also very fun!
>
> Love,
> Josh

Practice B on page 340.

Capital Letters, continued

■ Use a capital letter for each important word in the name of a special place.

Names of Special Places		
Streets West Avenue First Street	**Continents** Africa Asia	**Public Places** Central Park Piney Woods
Cities and States Dallas, Texas Miami, Florida	**Bodies of Water** Pacific Ocean Red River	**Buildings** Washington Monument Empire State Building
Countries Chile United States	**Landforms** Rocky Mountains Great Plains	**Planets** Earth Mars

■ Sometimes special place names are shortened, or abbreviated, but they still start with a capital letter.

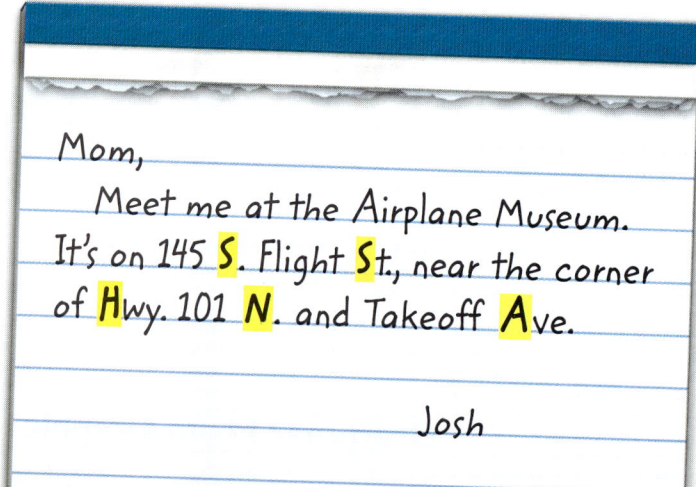

Practice C on page 342.

Use Adverbs in Writing

> Use **adverbs** to tell where, when, and how things happen. These details help make your writing clear and interesting.
>
> **Example:** Josh and Aunt Sue looked **carefully** at the exhibit in the Science Center.

Josh added adverbs to give important details.

The adverb **loudly** tells Grandma just how the dinosaur roared.

256 South Vista Drive
Silver City, Arizona
May 4, 2003

Dear Grandma,

 Yesterday I went with Aunt Sue to the Science Center. We go there every Saturday. There was a special dinosaur exhibit. Big robots showed how dinosaurs moved!

 You can control the robots with levers, just like a video game. When you press a button, the dinosaurs roar loudly. It was a little scary. It was also very fun!

 Love,
 Josh

Go To Practice B on page 340.

283

Capital Letters

> A word that begins with a **capital letter** is special in some way.
>
> Example: **O**ur class will go to the **N**ational **A**irplane **M**useum.

🟥 Use a capital letter to show where a sentence begins.

Examples: **W**e will take an exciting trip next **M**onday!

Our class will visit a museum with all kinds of airplanes.

🟥 Always write the word **I** with a capital letter.

Who is coming?

You and **I** can make a list.

🟥 Use a capital letter for a person's
- **first name**
- **last name**
- **initials**
- **title**.

Class Trip List

Students | Parents
Billy **R**oss | Mrs. Lane
Luisa Díaz | Ms. Kelly
J. J. Kelly | Dr. Díaz

Use these titles for people.
- **Mr.** for a man
- **Mrs.** for a married woman
- **Ms.** for any woman
- **Dr.** for a doctor

■ Begin the name of a day or a month with a capital letter. Also capitalize their abbreviations.

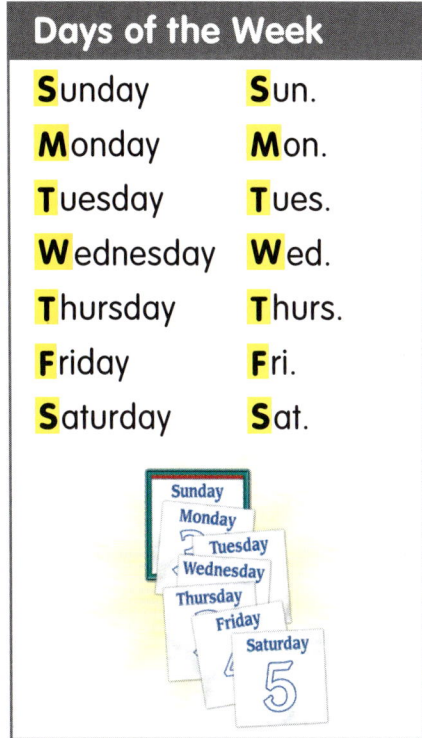

Days of the Week

Sunday	**S**un.
Monday	**M**on.
Tuesday	**T**ues.
Wednesday	**W**ed.
Thursday	**T**hurs.
Friday	**F**ri.
Saturday	**S**at.

Months of the Year

January	**J**an.
February	**F**eb.
March	**M**ar.
April	**A**pr.
May	
June	
July	
August	**A**ug.
September	**S**ept.
October	**O**ct.
November	**N**ov.
December	**D**ec.

These months are never abbreviated.

■ Begin each important word in the name of a special day or holiday with a capital letter.

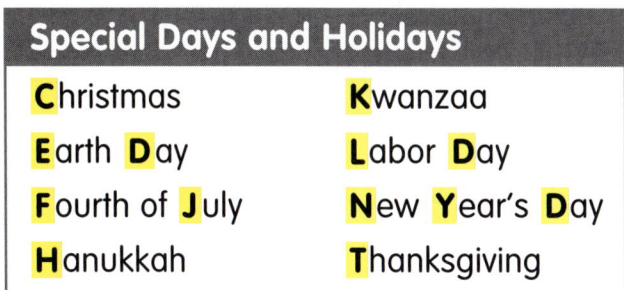

Special Days and Holidays

Christmas	**K**wanzaa
Earth **D**ay	**L**abor **D**ay
Fourth of **J**uly	**N**ew **Y**ear's **D**ay
Hanukkah	**T**hanksgiving

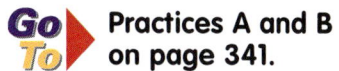 Practices A and B on page 341.

Grammar Made Graphic 285

Capital Letters, continued

■ Use a capital letter for each important word in the name of a special place.

Names of Special Places		
Streets West Avenue First Street	**Continents** Africa Asia	**Public Places** Central Park Piney Woods
Cities and States Dallas, Texas Miami, Florida	**Bodies of Water** Pacific Ocean Red River	**Buildings** Washington Monument Empire State Building
Countries Chile United States	**Landforms** Rocky Mountains Great Plains	**Planets** Earth Mars

■ Sometimes special place names are shortened, or abbreviated, but they still start with a capital letter.

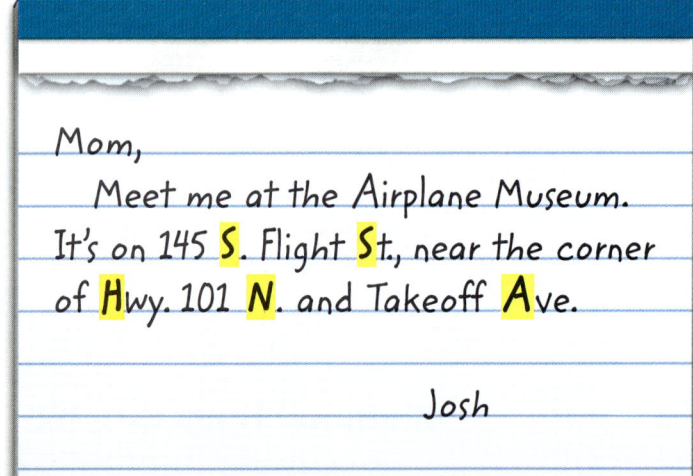

Practice C on page 342.

- When you write a person's exact words, begin the first word with a capital letter.

  Examples: Mrs. Ling said, "**T**ell me about the museum."

  J. J. answered, "**I**t had some old airplanes."

- Begin the greeting and the closing of a postcard or a letter with a capital letter.

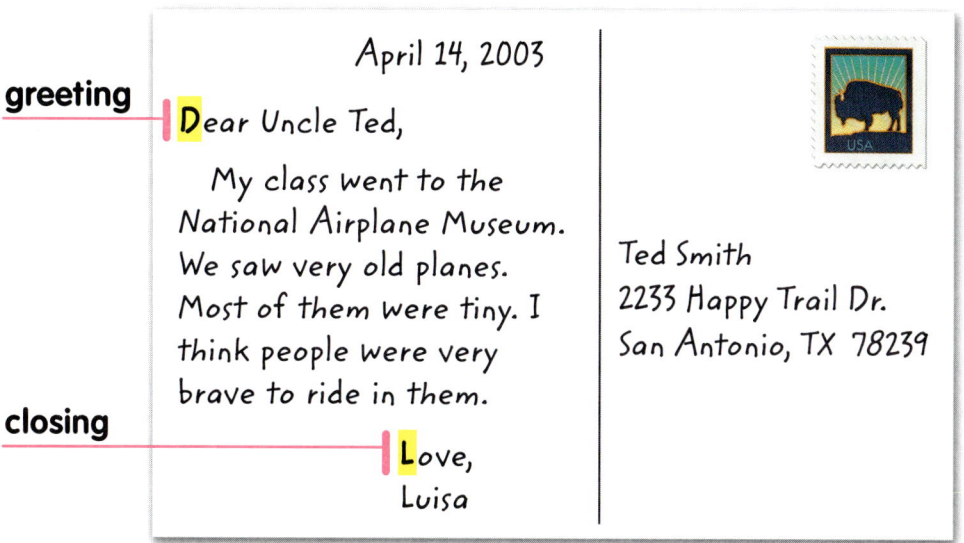

greeting — **D**ear Uncle Ted,

closing — **L**ove,

- Each important word in a book title starts with a capital letter.

Shaka's **L**ong **T**rip

Planes of the **P**ast

Punctuation Marks

Punctuation marks make words and sentences easier to understand.

- period
- question mark
- exclamation point
- comma
- quotation marks
- apostrophe

End Marks

■ Always use a punctuation mark at the end of a sentence.

•	Use a **period** when you tell something or give a polite command.	 "I have a new job at Downtown Car Sales." "Tell me about it, Uncle Dan."
?	Use a **question mark** when you ask a question.	 "What do you want to know, Mike?" "How many cars are for sale?"
!	Use an **exclamation point** to show strong feelings.	 "We have over 250 cars!" "Wow, that is a lot!"

Go To ▶ Practice A on page 344.

Grammar Made Graphic

More Ways to Use a Period

- Use a **period** after the abbreviation of a place or of a person's title.

  Mr. Blake works for Downtown Car Sales at 2456 N. Yale Ave. in Houston.

  BUT: When you address an envelope or postcard to mail, you abbreviate the state name differently. Capitalize both letters and do **not** use a period.

  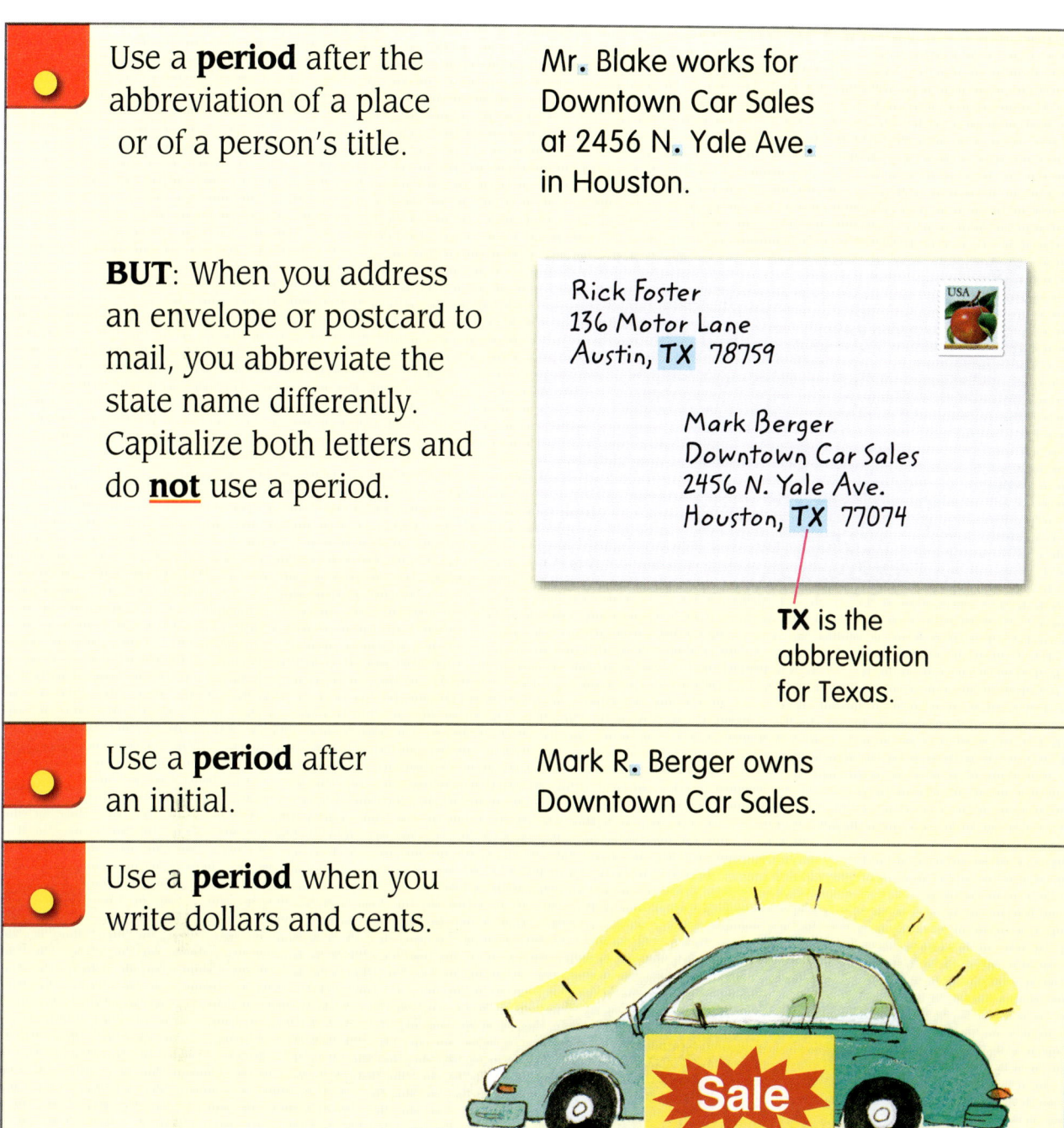

  TX is the abbreviation for Texas.

- Use a **period** after an initial.

  Mark R. Berger owns Downtown Car Sales.

- Use a **period** when you write dollars and cents.

  Sale — Save $900.00

The Comma

, Use **commas** when you write large numbers.

, Use **commas** when you write three or more items in a series.

Mr. Blake sells cars, vans, and trucks.

Sometimes he eats dinner, drives to work, and stays until 11 o'clock.

, Use a **comma** after short words like **Oh**, **Yes**, and **Well** when they come at the beginning of a sentence.

Oh, you work at night.

Well, that is when many people buy cars.

, You use **commas** a lot when you write a letter.

673 Hill Street
Chico, CA 95926
July 7, 2002

Dear Monika,
　Today I watched Uncle Dan sell cars. Mrs. Palmer picked out a red car. Then Uncle Dan took me to lunch. We had a great day!

　　　Your friend,
　　　Mike

Use a comma
- between the city and state
- between the day and the year
- after the greeting
- after the closing.

Grammar Made Graphic

,	Use a **comma** before **and**, **but**, or **or** in a compound sentence.	Mike visited Uncle Dan at work**,** **and** his uncle showed him all the cars. Mike watched Uncle Dan work**,** **but** he had to be quiet. Mike could go home for lunch**,** **or** he could go to a restaurant with his uncle.
,	Use a **comma** before the exact words of a speaker.	Mike said**,** "Thanks for taking me to work." His uncle said**,** "You are welcome."

 Practices C and D on pages 344–345.

Quotation Marks

" "	Use **quotation marks** to show the exact words of a speaker.	Mrs. Palmer wanted to show her new car to her children. **"**I have a surprise for you,**"** Mrs. Palmer said. The children went outside. They saw the new car! **"**It is beautiful,**"** said Pam. Diane said, **"**I want to take a ride right now!**"**

Go To Practice E on page 345.

Grammar Made Graphic

The Apostrophe

9 Use an **apostrophe** to show that a person or thing owns something.

- Use **'s** to show that one person or thing owns something.
- Use **s'** to show that two or more people own something.
- Use **'s** when a plural noun does not end in **s**.

9 A **contraction** is a short form of two words. Every contraction has an **apostrophe**. It shows that one or more letters have been left out.

"**I'm** going to take you for a ride," said Mom. They **couldn't** wait to go! "**Don't** forget your seatbelts," she said.

After a while, Mom asked, "**Who's** ready for a snack? **Here's** an apple."

"**That's** a good snack," said Molly.

Grammar Made Graphic

9

You can make a contraction from a verb and the word **not**. Shorten **not** to **n't**.

is not = isn't   does not = doesn't
are not = aren't   did not = didn't
was not = wasn't   has not = hasn't
were not = weren't   have not = haven't
do not = don't   could not = couldn't

Spelling Tip

Some contractions have special spellings.

will not = won't
can not = can't

You can make a contraction from a pronoun or some other words and a verb. Shorten the verb.

I am = I'm   who is = who's
you are = you're   here is = here's
he is = he's   you will = you'll
she is = she's   he will = he'll
it is = it's   she will = she'll
we are = we're   it will = it'll
they are = they're   we will = we'll
there is = there's   they will = they'll

Grammar Tip

Don't confuse **it's** and **its**.

<u>it's</u> = it is
<u>its</u> is a pronoun

It's a very nice car.
Its stereo sounds really good!

Go To Practice F on page 345.

Grammar Made Graphic 293

How do you turn questions into answers? Get the facts! Look things up in the library or on the Internet. Talk to people. Take notes. Share what you learn!

The Research Process

When you **research**, you look for information about something. You can use the information you find to give a talk, tell a story, or write a research report.

STEP 1 Choose a Topic

Think of something you want to learn about. This is your research **topic**.

STEP 2 Think of Questions

Make a list of research questions about your topic.

Find the **key words** in your questions. Look up these words when you start your research.

Look It Up!

STEP
3 Find Information

You can use different **resources** to find information about your topic.

books

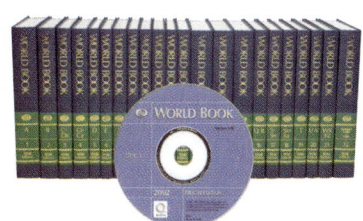
encyclopedias

Internet

magazines

expert

An **expert** is someone who knows a lot about a topic.

You can start your research in a library. See pages 298–299 to find out more about a library.

Look It Up!

Library

A library is a place that has many books, magazines, and other **resources**. It is organized in a special way to help you find things.

If you cannot find something, ask for help at the **Information Desk**.

One part of the library has **nonfiction** books. They have information about different topics.

The **Children's Room** has books for children.

The **card catalog** lists the books and other materials in the library. Most libraries have their card catalog on computer, too.

Look It Up!

Re**search**

The **Reference Section** has special books like dictionaries and encyclopedias.

Dictionary

Encyclopedia

The **Checkout Desk** is where you **check out**, or take home, books.

Magazines have articles in them. Most magazines are published every week or month.

You can use the library's **computers** to find information on the Internet.

Look It Up!

STEP
4 Take Notes

When you do research, write down important words and ideas. These **notes** help you remember the information.

■ First set up your notecards.

Write your **research question** at the top.

■ Find a good **source** of information.

This book is an example of a **source**.

300 Look It Up!

■ Find the page with the information you need.

■ Write the **source** on your notecard.

Write the **title** and underline it.

Write the **author**.

Write the **page number**.

Now you are ready to take notes.

Look It Up! 301

❹ Take Notes, continued

■ Write notes in **your own words**.

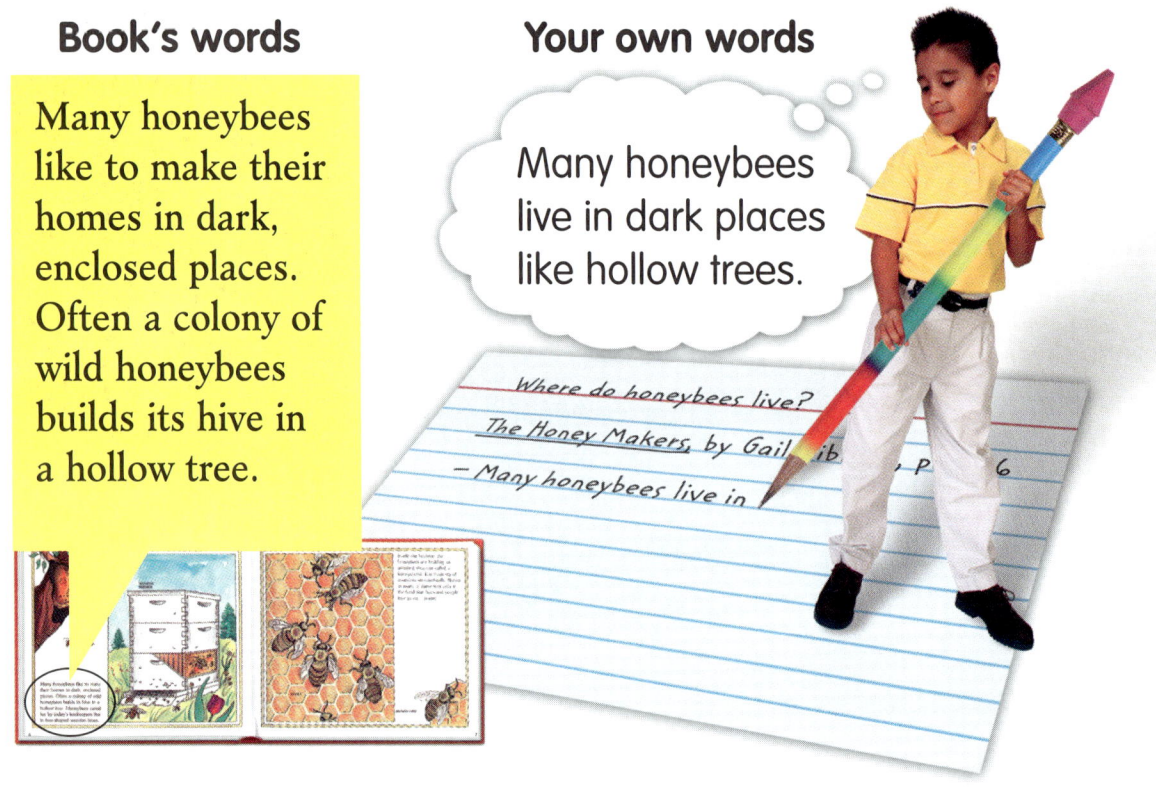

■ If you copy what you read, put **quotation marks** around the words.

> Where do honeybees live?
>
> The Honey Makers, by Gail Gibbons, page 6
>
> — Many honeybees live in dark places like hollow trees.
>
> — "Honeybees cared for by today's beekeepers live in box-shaped wooden hives."

■ Draw diagrams or other pictures that go with your notes.

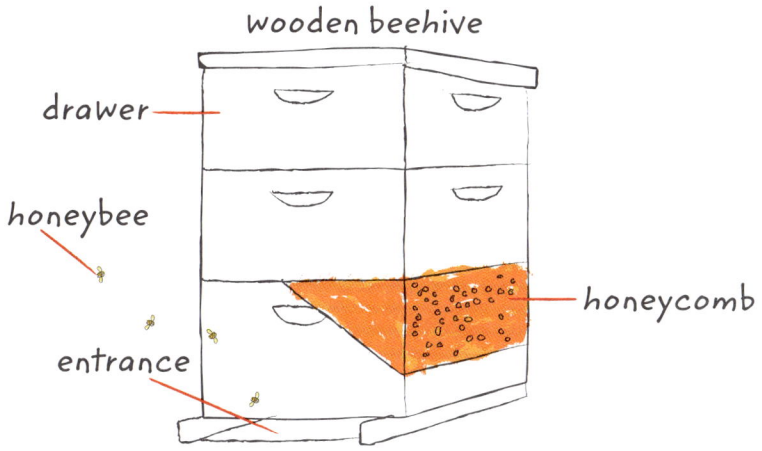

■ Think about the information, and ask new questions. Look for more answers.

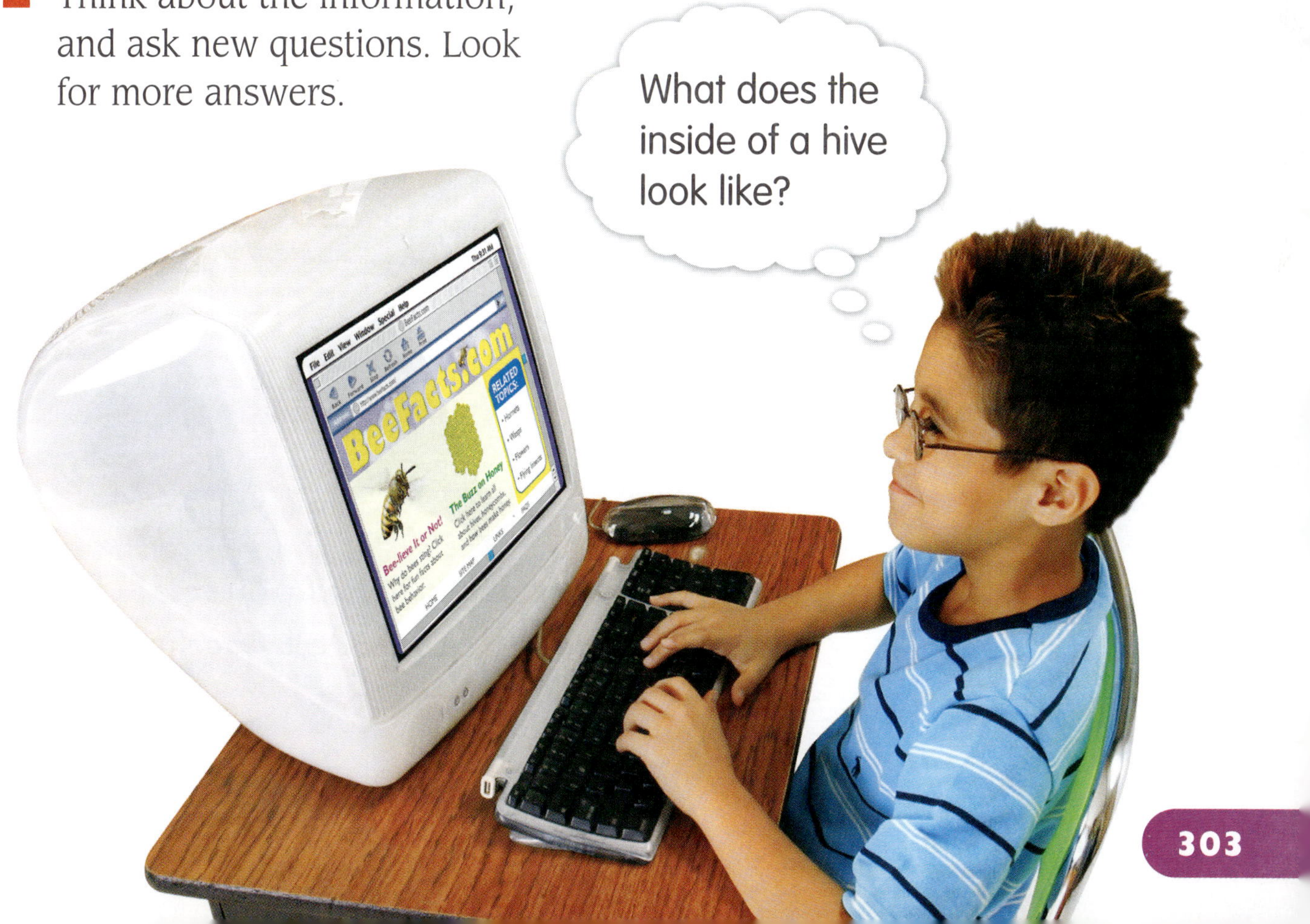

What does the inside of a hive look like?

STEP
5 Make an Outline

Turn your notes into an **outline**. An outline is a plan for writing your report.

■ Look at your notecards. Group the cards for each research question.

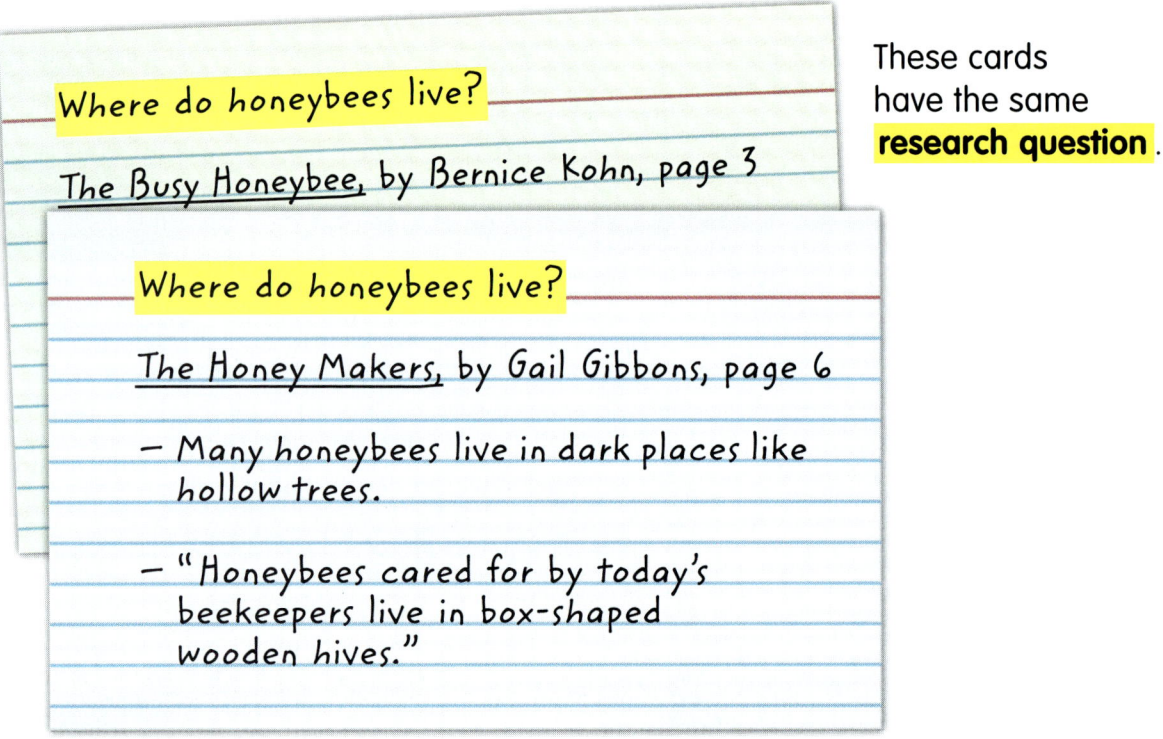

These cards have the same **research question**.

■ Turn your notes into an outline.

Turn each question into a **main idea**.

Then list **details** from your notes.

I. Where honeybees live
  A. Dark places like hollow trees
  B. Wooden boxes made by beekeepers

- Here is an example of a finished outline.

A **Roman numeral** comes before each **main idea**.

A **capital letter** comes before each **detail**.

Honeybees and Honey

I. Where honeybees live
   A. Dark places like hollow trees
   B. Wooden boxes made by beekeepers

II. Inside the hives
   A. Sometimes more than 50,000 bees
   B. Mostly worker bees
   C. Honeycombs

III. How honeybees make honey
   A. Gather nectar from flowers
   B. Store nectar in cells
   C. Fan nectar with wings
   D. Nectar becomes honey

- Think about what you learned. Write down any new questions. You can go back to answer those questions now or later.

Look It Up!

STEP 6 # Turn Your Research into a Report

Now you are ready to write a **research report**. Turn the main ideas and details from your outline into sentences and paragraphs.

▪ Look at the **title** of your outline. Can you make it more interesting for your report?

Outline

Honeybees and Honey

Title of report

Sweet Treats from Bees

▪ Next, write an **introduction**. It is the first paragraph of your report. The introduction should be interesting. It should tell what your report is mostly about.

Introduction

Sweet Treats from Bees

Can you imagine a house full of honey? You can if you know about honeybees.

Look It Up!

■ For the next paragraph, look at **Roman numeral I** on your outline. Turn this main idea into a **topic sentence**. Use the **important words** in a complete sentence.

Outline

Honeybees and Honey

I. Where honeybees live

Introduction

Sweet Treats from Bees

Can you imagine a house full of honey? You can if you know about honeybees.

Topic sentence

Honeybees live and make honey in different kinds of hives.

Look It Up!

6 Turn Your Research into a Report, continued

■ Look at letters **A** and **B**. Turn these **details** into sentences that tell more about the main idea. Add them to your paragraph.

Outline

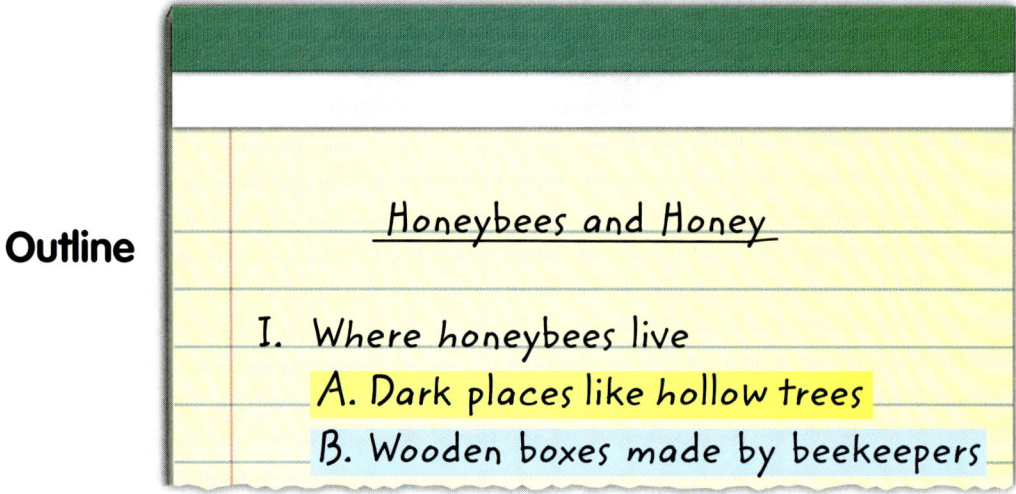

Introduction

Sweet Treats from Bees

Can you imagine a house full of honey? You can if you know about honeybees.

First paragraph

Honeybees live and make honey in different kinds of hives. A hive is a home for bees. Some honeybees build hives in hollow trees and in other dark places. Other honeybees live in wooden boxes made by beekeepers.

■ Write a paragraph for each Roman numeral on your outline.

308 Look It Up!

■ Write a **conclusion**, or a summary of the most important information. The conclusion is the last paragraph. Look back at all the **main ideas** on your outline. Put them in your conclusion.

Outline

Honeybees and Honey

I. Where honeybees live
   A. Dark places like hollow trees
   B. Wooden boxes made by beekeepers

II. Inside the hives
   A. Sometimes more than 50,000 bees
   B. Mostly worker bees
   C. Honeycombs

III. How honeybees make honey
   A. Gather nectar from flowers
   B. Store nectar in cells
   C. Fan nectar with wings
   D. Nectar becomes honey

Conclusion

Honeybee hives are busy homes. Many honeybees work together to make and store honey inside their hives. Honeybees turn nectar from flowers into a sweet treat to eat.

Look It Up!

STEP 7 Put It All Together!

Use pages 114–121 of **The Writing Process** to revise, proofread, and publish your research report. Include pictures, diagrams, graphs, or charts to explain information.

The <mark>title</mark> and <mark>introduction</mark> tell what your report is about. They get your reader interested.

The **body** of the report presents the facts you found.

Diagrams help your reader understand.

Sweet Treats from Bees

Can you imagine a house full of honey? You can if you know about honeybees.

Honeybees live and make honey in different kinds of hives. A hive is a home for bees. Some honeybees build hives in hollow trees and in other dark places. Other honeybees live in wooden boxes made by beekeepers.

It is crowded and busy inside a honeybee hive. A hive can have more than 50,000 honeybees. Most of them are worker bees. They build wax honeycombs that have thousands of small parts called cells. Worker bees store honey in most of the cells.

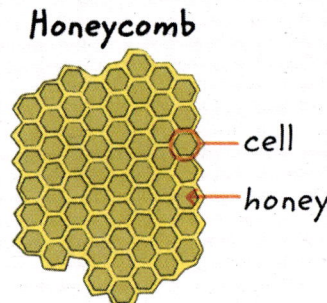

310 Look It Up!

Re**search**

It takes a lot of work to make honey! First, worker bees gather nectar from flowers. Nectar is a sweet liquid. The bees drink it. Then they return to the hive and spit up the nectar. Other worker bees store the nectar in cells. They fan the nectar with their wings to dry it out. The nectar gets thick and becomes honey for the bees to eat.

Honeybee hives are busy homes. Many honeybees work together to make and store honey inside their hives. Honeybees turn nectar from flowers into a sweet treat to eat.

Each paragraph in the body begins with a **topic sentence**. It tells a main idea. The other sentences give details.

The last paragraph is the **conclusion**. It sums up the report.

Resource Tools

Books

Most nonfiction books have special parts at the front and back. These parts help you know what the book is about and how to find information in it.

Title Page

The **title page** is usually the first page in a book.

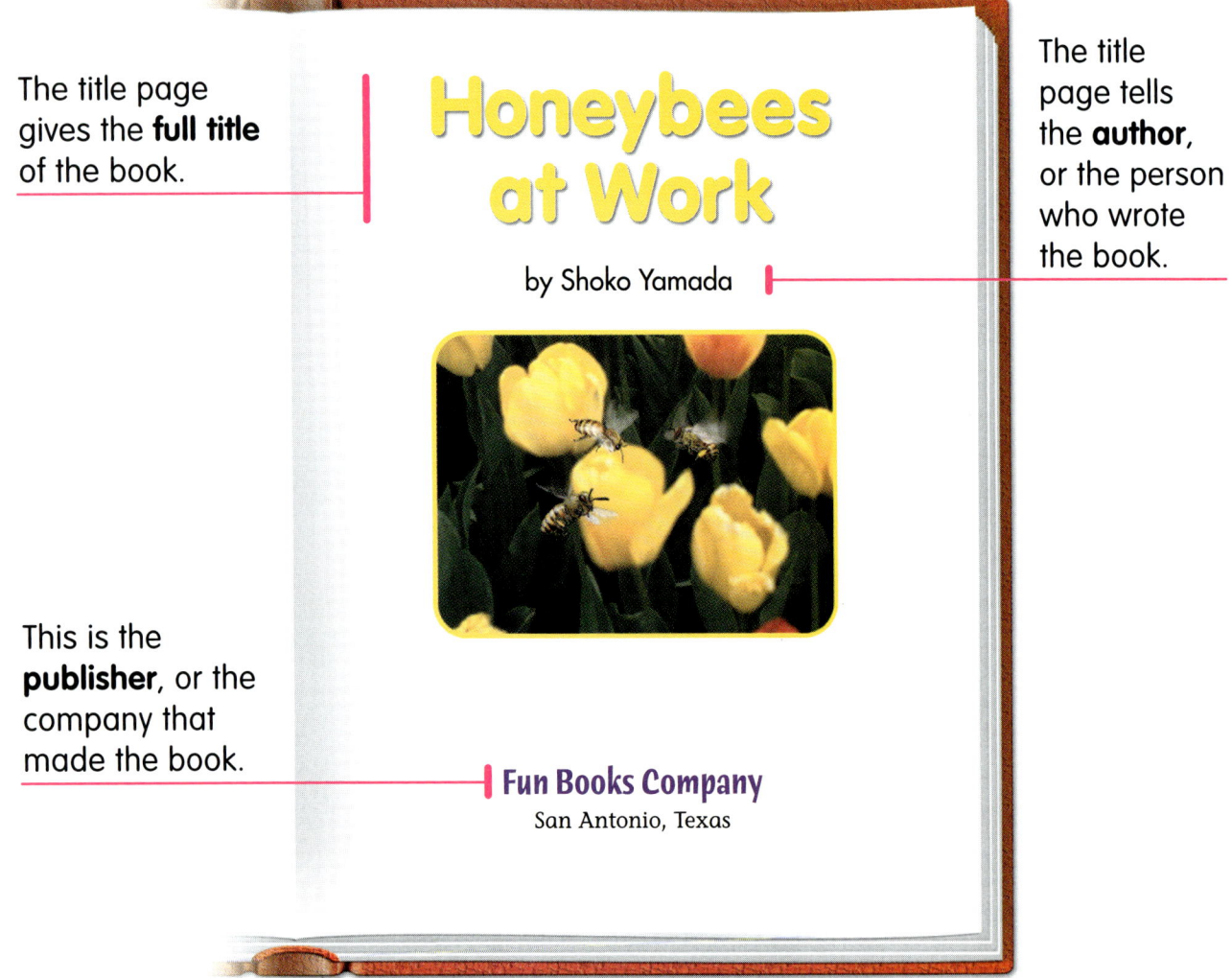

The title page gives the **full title** of the book.

The title page tells the **author**, or the person who wrote the book.

This is the **publisher**, or the company that made the book.

Table of Contents

Some books have a **table of contents** after the title page. The table of contents lists the **chapters**, or main parts, of a book.

Table of Contents

Chapter	Page
1. Kinds of Hives	5
2. Honeycombs	12
3. How Honey is Made	17
4. Worker Bees	23
5. Queen Bee	31
Glossary	34
Internet Sites	37
Index	40

The **chapter title** tells what the chapter is mostly about.

The **page number** tells what page the chapter begins on.

Glossary

A **glossary** is a short dictionary. It **defines**, or tells the meaning of, important words in a book. It appears near the end of the book.

The words are in alphabetical order by their **first letter**.

If words have the same first letter, look at the **second letter**.

Glossary

beekeeper — a person who raises bees for their honey

cell — a small, hollow place

colony — a large number of bees living together

hive — a structure where bees live

honey — a sweet, sticky liquid that bees make

honeybee — a bee that makes honey

honeycomb — a group of wax cells built by honeybees in their hive

Look It Up!

Index

The **index** is at the back of a book. It tells where to find important ideas and words in the book.

The **entries**, or key words, are arranged in alphabetical order.

The **page numbers** tell where to look in the book for information about an entry.

Index

adult bees, 23
beekeeper, 21
colony, 6, 8, 23, 31
defense, 24
eggs, 31
flowers, 17, 19
food, 21
hives, 5, 12, 23
honey, 5, 15, 17, 19, 23, 32

honeybees, 5, 7, 9, 11, 13, 15, 17, 20
honeycomb, 12, 14, 21
nectar, 17, 19, 21
pollen, 18, 24
queen bee, 31
wax, 13
worker bees, 23, 25, 28

Look It Up!

Encyclopedia

An **encyclopedia** is a set of reference books with facts about many different topics. Each book is called a **volume**. The volumes are in alphabetical order.

How to Find Information in an Encyclopedia

 What is the first letter of the word you want to look up? Find the volume for that letter. For example, if your topic is **rain forests**, look in the **R** volume.

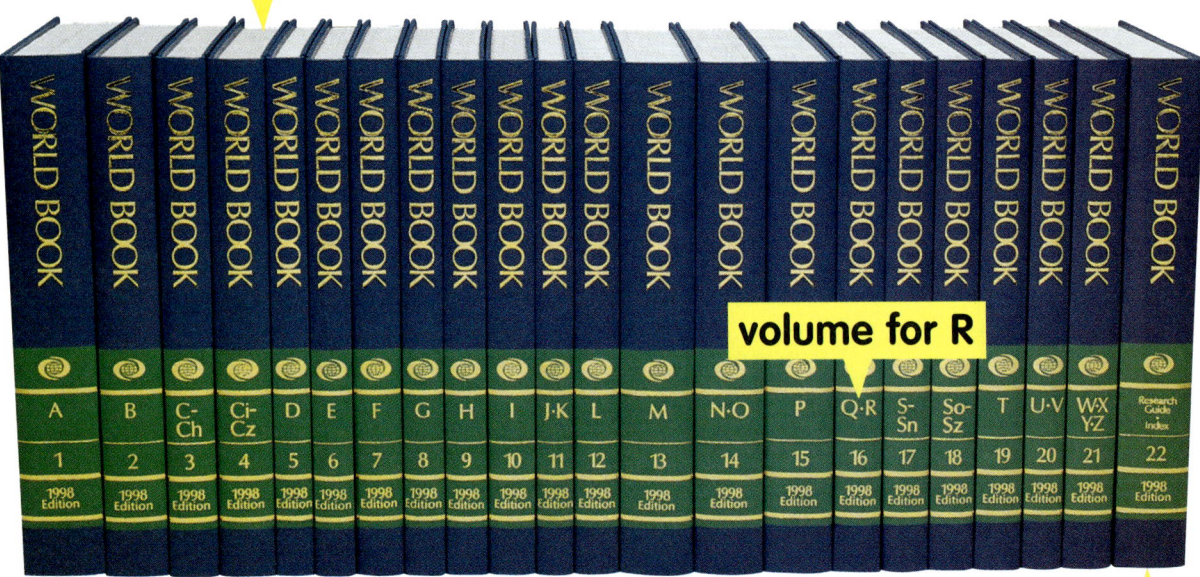

Most encyclopedias have a volume called an **index**. It lists other key words you can look up to find information about your topic.

316   Look It Up!

2 Use alphabetical order to look up your word.

Some encyclopedias are on a computer disk called a **CD-ROM**. You can read the information from the CD-ROM on your computer screen.

Look It Up! **317**

Experts

An **expert** is someone who knows a lot about a topic. Ask questions, or **interview**, an expert to get answers about your topic.

Interviewing Tips

- ✓ Write down the questions you want to ask.
- ✓ Think of someone who might know a lot about your topic.
- ✓ Ask the person if he or she has time to answer your questions.
- ✓ Ask your questions clearly and politely.
- ✓ Listen carefully and take notes.
- ✓ Ask more questions if you do not understand something.
- ✓ Say thank you.

Magazines

Look for articles about your topic in magazines. Most magazines are published every week or month. Each magazine is called an **issue**.

The **magazine title** is on each issue.

The **date** tells when the issue was published.

These are some of the **topics** in the issue.

This is the **main topic** in the issue.

Look It Up!   319

Internet

The **Internet** is a connection of computers that share information through the **World Wide Web**. You can find information on the Internet.

How to Do Research on the Web

❶ Click twice on an **icon** to get into the Internet. An icon is a picture on your computer screen.

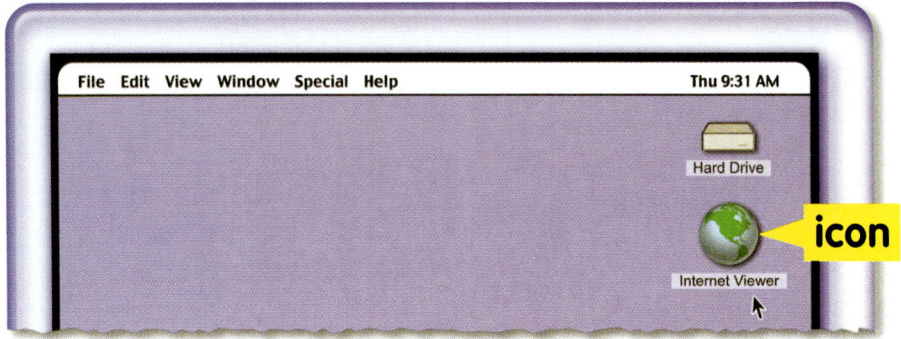

❷ Go to a **search page**. Type your key words in the search box. Then click on **Search**.

This is a **toolbar**. Click on the pictures to do what they say.

Type your key words here.

Click here to **search**, or look for, your key words.

3 Read the list of **Web sites**, or pages, that have your key words. The underlined words are **links** to the Web sites.

Read the descriptions carefully. This site may be interesting, but it may not help you with your report.

4 Click on a link to go directly to the **site**, or **Web page**. If you want to go back to the list of Web sites, click on the **back arrow**.

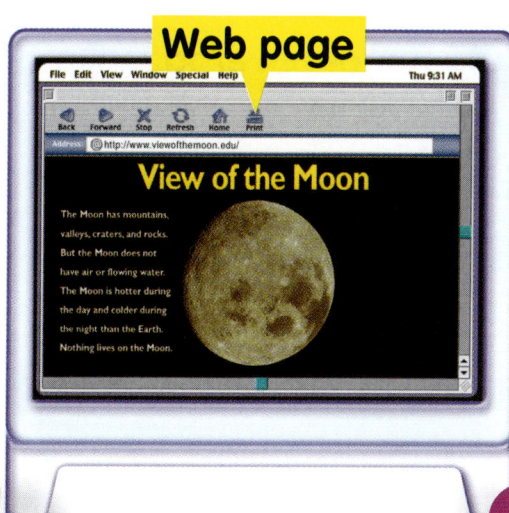

Grammar Practice

Sentences

A. Finish each sentence. Use an ending from the box. Write the sentence.

all weekend.	come to the city?	can see a movie.
say it's okay!	Friday night!	I come?
your parents.	movies!	to get there!

question   1. Can you ____

statement   2. We ____

exclamation   3. Wow, I love ____

question   4. When can ____

command   5. Come on ____

statement   6. I can stay ____

command   7. First, ask ____

exclamation   8. They ____

exclamation   9. I can't wait ____

B. Add *not* or *never* to make a negative sentence. Write the sentence.

1. Tomás walks to school. He ____ rides the bus.

2. He is ____ here this morning.

3. He was ____ at school yesterday.

4. He ____ misses school. I hope he is okay.

C. Add a subject. Write the sentence.

1. _____ plays with his dog in the park.
   subject   predicate

2. _____ walks on a leash.
   subject   predicate

3. _____ are in the park, too.
   subject   predicate

D. Add a predicate. Write the sentence.

1. Mom _____
   subject   predicate

2. The children _____
   subject   predicate

3. The brown dog _____
   subject   predicate

Grammar Practice

Grammar Practice

E. **Write each compound sentence. Use the correct word.**

1. Anna visits Granny, __and / but__ they go to the street fair.

2. They want to take a cab, __or / but__ it costs too much.

3. "We can take a bus, __or / and__ we can walk," says Granny.

4. "I like to walk, __and / but__ it is too far," says Anna.

5. Soon a bus comes, __and / or__ they get on.

6. "Do you want to sit here, __but / or__ do you like the window seat?" Granny asks.

F. **Join the sentences. Use a word from the box. Write the new sentence.**

and	but	or

1. At the fair, Granny plays games. Anna goes on rides.

2. Granny has plain popcorn. Anna asks for popcorn with butter.

3. The next day they can come back to the fair. They can go to the movies.

Nouns

A. Write these sentences. Add the correct nouns.

| lake | Anna | people | ducks | Park Street |

1. ____ takes a walk with her father.
2. They walk to ____ .
3. They see many ____ in the stores.
4. Then they walk by a ____ in the park.
5. Anna watches the ____ in the water.

B. Copy the chart. Write the plural of each noun in the second column. Then draw a picture to go with each noun.

	One	More than One
1.	book	
2.	bowl	
3.	dish	
4.	cake	
5.	penny	
6.	foot	
7.	berry	
8.	child	

Grammar Practice

Grammar Practice

C. Choose the correct word to complete each sentence. Write the sentence.

1. Efram's family wants to hear ___a / an___ concert.
2. They see ___a / an___ ad for a concert.
3. They decide to go to ___an / the___ concert that night.
4. The family rides ___a / an___ bus that goes to the city.
5. It takes almost ___a / an___ hour to get there!
6. Efram wants to sit close to ___an / the___ stage.
7. ___The / A___ music sounds great!

D. Write these sentences. Use the correct possessive noun.

1. Kay has a bike. ___Kay's / Kays'___ bike is brand new.
2. Kay has two brothers. Her ___brother's / brothers'___ bikes are not new.
3. One ___boy's / boys___ bike has a flat tire.
4. Mr. Bill will fix the ___bikes' / bike's___ tire.

E. Write the paragraph. Replace the underlined words with precise nouns. Tell about your city or town.

Let's take a walk down <u>the street</u>. We will smell delicious <u>food</u> at <u>the restaurant</u>. Maybe <u>people</u> will play <u>music</u> on the sidewalk. We will see many beautiful <u>things</u> in the windows of <u>the store</u>. We will have fun in <u>this town</u>.

Pronouns

A. Write these sentences.
Use the correct pronoun.

1. Aunt Sue comes to the city.
   ___She___ visits Clare and Ray.

2. Clare shows Aunt Sue a bedroom.
   "___You___ can sleep here," Clare says.

3. Ray and Clare show Aunt Sue the city.
   ___They___ all take a walk.

4. Aunt Sue takes the children into the library.
   "___We___ will each get a book," Aunt Sue says.

5. Ray checks out a book to read.
   ___He___ also checks out one for Aunt Sue.

6. Clare points outside.
   "___I___ see a man selling pretzels," Clare says.

7. Aunt Sue buys some pretzels.
   ___They___ are warm and salty.

8. Ray points to a bench.
   "___We___ can sit and eat," Ray says.

Grammar Practice 327

Grammar Practice

**B. Write these sentences.
Use the correct pronoun.**

1. Clare and Ray paint pictures of ____their / they____ town.
2. Clare draws ____she / her____ house.
3. She shows ____its / it____ front yard.
4. She does not have red paint for the flowers. "May I use ____you / your____ red paint?" she asks Ray.
5. Ray draws ____her / his____ school.
6. "Here is ____I / my____ teacher," Ray says.
7. "We can send the pictures to ____we / our____ grandparents," Clare says.
8. Grandma and Grandpa like the pictures. They put the pictures on ____their / its____ wall.

**C. Write these sentences.
Use the correct pronoun.**

1. We clean up our neighborhood. There is a job for each of ____us / our____ .
2. Clare and Ray are there. The leader asks ____they / them____ to rake the leaves.
3. Dad wants a job, too. "What do you want ____me / I____ to do?" he asks.
4. We tell ____he / him____ to put the leaves in a bag.
5. Dad fills the bag and carries ____it / them____ to the truck.

Subject Pronouns	Object Pronouns
I	me
you	you
he, she, it	him, her, it
we	us
they	them

328 Grammar Practice

D. Write these sentences. Use the correct word.

1. __This / These__ park needs to be cleaned up.
2. __That / Those__ girls will plant flowers.
3. I will paint __that / this__ bench over there.
4. Put the trash in __these / this__ bags.
5. __These / This__ neighborhood has a great park!

E. Write the paragraph. Replace the underlined words with the correct pronoun.

The neighbors on our block want to have a party. The neighbors want to have the party this weekend! Mrs. Brown is knocking on all the doors. Mrs. Brown is asking people to prepare a dish. Everyone likes Mrs. Brown, so they all say "yes." The party is going to be a great party!

Grammar Practice

Grammar Practice

Adjectives

A. Write these sentences. Add an adjective. Choose one from the box or think of one yourself.

1. The train passed through the ____ mountains.
2. All the cars were ____.
3. The train looked like a ____ snake.
4. It went over a ____ bridge.
5. At night, you could see the train's ____ light.

clean	tall
bright	shiny
long	red
low	big
high	white

B. Write these sentences. Add an adjective from the box.

1. There are so ____ cars in this train!
2. It has about ____ cars.
3. ____ trains have more cars.
4. ____ engine drives the train.
5. It does not take ____ time to get to the city.

| thirty |
| much |
| One |
| Some |
| many |

C. Write these sentences. Use the correct adjective to make a comparison.

1. Bicycles are __slower / slowest__ than cars.

2. Of all the ways to travel, rockets are the __faster / fastest__.

3. Trucks can carry __heavier / heaviest__ loads than cars.

4. Trucks are __noisier / noisiest__ than cars.

5. Bikes are the __quieter / quietest__ of all.

6. Big cities have the __busier / busiest__ streets of any place.

7. For the __cleaner / cleanest__ bike, scrub with soap and water.

8. I think blue is a __prettier / prettiest__ color for a car than black.

Grammar Practice

Grammar Practice

D. Write these sentences. Use the correct adjective to make a comparison.

1. This road goes through the beautifulest / most beautiful part of town.

2. My most favorite / most favoritest part is the bridge.

3. You can see the best / goodest view from there.

4. The road is bumpy, but it is more good / better than Ford Road.

5. Traffic is worse / more worse there.

6. Ford Road is also more dangerous / dangerouser because it is curvy.

7. The baddest / worst time to drive is when the road is wet.

8. The more important / most important thing of all is to go slowly.

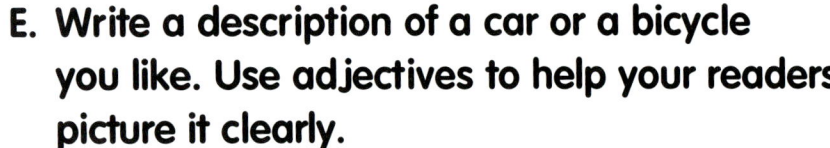

E. Write a description of a car or a bicycle you like. Use adjectives to help your readers picture it clearly.

Verbs

A. Write each sentence. Add a verb from the box.

1. We ____ at the playground.
2. The sun ____ hot.
3. I ____ on the swings.
4. My sister ____ at the pond.
5. My friends ____ on the slide.
6. Elena ____ at the top.
7. Mark ____ on the ladder.
8. They ____ happy!

> am
> are
> is

B. Write each sentence. Use the correct verb.

1. We ____ (have / has) soccer practice on Saturday morning.
2. The coach ____ (have / has) two helpers.
3. Each helper ____ (have / has) a group of kids.
4. The kids ____ (have / has) one hour to practice.
5. Then we ____ (have / has) one hour to play a game.
6. When we get home, Mom ____ (have / has) lunch ready.
7. We ____ (have / has) so much fun on Saturday morning!

Grammar Practice 333

Grammar Practice

C. Write each sentence. Use the correct verb.

1. I __play / plays__ baseball every day.
2. I __pitch / pitches__ the ball to Sam.
3. He __hit / hits__ the ball.
4. Then he __runs / run__ to a base.
5. Lisa __catch / catches__ the ball.
6. She __throw / throws__ the ball to me.
7. Sam __tries / try__ to run to the next base.
8. I __tag / tags__ him. Sam is out.
9. We __wins / win__ the game.
10. We __cheer / cheers__ for our team.

D. Write each sentence. Add the correct form of the red verb.

play	1. We ____ soccer after school.
shout	2. The coach ____ to the players.
watch	3. My dad ____ the game.
hurry	4. Berto ____ after the ball.
kick	5. He ____ the ball to me.
score	6. I ____ a goal.
wave	7. My dad ____ to me.
bark	8. My dog ____.
clap	9. My friends ____.
jump	10. We ____ up and down.

Grammar Practice 335

Grammar Practice

E. **Make a chart. Write each underlined verb in the correct column.**

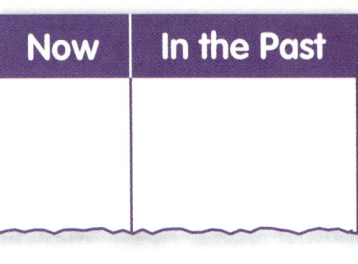

1. Pablo and I like soccer.
2. Yesterday we biked to the park.
3. We played a good game of soccer.
4. Today Pablo calls me on the phone.
5. I hurry over to Pablo's house.
6. We watch a good game of soccer on T.V.

F. **Write each sentence. Add -ed to change the underlined verb to the past tense.**

1. I walk to baseball practice.
2. I chase each ball.
3. I rush around the field.
4. I jump up to make a catch.
5. After practice, I rest!

G. Write each sentence. Change the underlined verb to the past tense. Use the chart to help you.

1. I <u>go</u> to the pool every day.
2. I <u>bring</u> my friend Mai.
3. Mai <u>knows</u> how to swim.
4. We <u>take</u> our lunch to the pool.
5. First, Mai <u>dives</u> into the pool.
6. Then, she <u>holds</u> her breath from one end of the pool to the other.
7. Next, Mai <u>does</u> the backstroke.
8. We <u>keep</u> busy all day.
9. The lifeguard <u>sees</u> us in the water.
10. He <u>says</u>, "Good work!"

Now	In the Past
bring	brought
dive	dove
do	did
go	went
keep	kept
know	knew
say	said
see	saw
take	took

Grammar Practice 337

Grammar Practice

H. Write each sentence. Use the correct verb.

1. I __was / were__ at the pool all day yesterday.
2. My friend and I __was / were__ there to practice for the race.
3. I __was / were__ glad to have my friend with me.
4. Other people from school __was / were__ there, too.
5. But they __was / were__ not there all day, like us!
6. The water __was / were__ cold at first, but we got used to it.
7. When we left, we __was / were__ really tired.
8. Our fingers __was / were__ all wrinkled from the water.

I. Write each sentence. Use the correct verb.

1. Every night I __listen / listened__ to the news, and I find out about the weather.
2. Yesterday it __snow / snowed__ a lot.
3. All the kids __stay / stayed__ home from school.
4. Tomorrow the sun __shined / is going to shine__.
5. The sun __melted / will melt__ the snow.
6. When the snow is gone, we __will play / played__ in the park.

J. Write each statement or question. Use the correct verb.

1. We __is / are__ going to the park today.
2. __Do / Does__ you want to play?
3. You __is / can__ be on my team.
4. __Is / Are__ Tina throwing the ball to Felipe?
5. Yes. He __might / am__ catch it.
6. __Is / Are__ he jumping up to get it?
7. I __are / am__ reaching for it, too.
8. My friends __are / is__ shouting at me!
9. I __does / do__ not drop it. I catch it!
10. __Does / Do__ my team cheer? Yes, they do!

K. Write two or three sentences about a sport or an outdoor activity that you like. Use colorful verbs.

Grammar Practice

Adverbs

A. Write these sentences. Add an adverb. Choose one from the box or think of one yourself.

1. Josh and Aunt Sue went to the science museum _____ .
2. They saw dinosaurs _____ .
3. The dinosaurs roared _____ !
4. Josh _____ realized that the dinosaurs were just robots.

| loudly |
| there |
| quickly |
| today |

---

5. Josh and Aunt Sue wandered _____ .
6. They studied every exhibit _____ .
7. Aunt Sue _____ said it was time to go.
8. Josh _____ loves to visit the science museum!

| around |
| finally |
| always |
| carefully |

B. Write a paragraph about a visit to a museum, a circus, or some other interesting place. Use adverbs to tell when, where, and how.

Capital Letters

A. Write each sentence. Use capital letters correctly.

1. a pilot came to mrs. Smith's class.
2. his name was Captain charles worth.
3. the children had many questions for Captain Worth.
4. Betty jasper and i asked how long it took to learn to fly.
5. some kids wanted to know if it is hard to fly.

B. Write each sentence. Use capital letters correctly.

1. Betty's family took an airplane trip in may.
2. They flew on memorial day.
3. The holiday was on a monday.
4. They will go again on labor day.
5. That will be in september.
6. They will be there on saturday, sunday, and monday.

Grammar Practice

C. Write each sentence. Use capital letters correctly.

1. The class visited Captain Worth at central airport.
2. The airport is on elm st. in boulder city.
3. The pilot flies in canada and in the united states.
4. "This afternoon, I will fly from california to ohio," he said.
5. "I love to see the pacific ocean from the air," the pilot said.

D. Write this letter. Use capital letters correctly.

E. Write this list of book titles. Use capital letters correctly.

1. *first book of airplanes*
2. *become a pilot*
3. *taro takes a ride*
4. *airplanes, helicopters, and balloons*
5. *history of travel*
6. *mystery at midtown airport*

F. Write each sentence. Use capital letters correctly.

1. betty took a trip with john, her uncle, to shell beach.
2. they rented a boat and went to turtle island.
3. ms. king gave them a book called *boat safety*.
4. they paddled around oak bay.
5. john said, "it is hot for early june."
6. betty said, "we can stop at the island and sit under a tree."

Grammar Practice

Grammar Practice

Punctuation

A. Write each sentence. Add the correct punctuation at the end.

1. What job does your mother do
2. She drives a truck for a flower shop
3. Please take these flowers to the hospital
4. Wow, what a great job I have

B. Write each sentence. Add periods where they belong.

1. Mom's boss is J W Daffodil.
2. Mr Daffodil is a very nice man.
3. He charges $27 50 for a bunch of roses.

C. Write the following letter. Add commas where they are needed.

Flores Flower Shop
10 Major Lane
Chester Maryland   21009
August 5 2003

Dear Mrs. Flores
You take good care of the flowers. You drive safely. Thank you for doing a great job.
    Sincerely
    Marcos

D. Write each sentence. Add commas where they are needed.

1. Mr. Waters used to own a restaurant but now he owns a gas station.
2. Mr. Waters sells gas oil snacks and soft drinks.
3. Well he also sells newspapers and maps.
4. The station opens at 8:00 in the morning and Mr. Waters spends all day there.

E. Write the following sentences. Add commas and quotation marks where they are needed.

1. I want to buy a truck said Dad.
2. Mike answered A truck is useful!
3. Yes, I can carry things said Dad.
4. Dad told Mike You can pick the color of the truck.
5. Mike said OK. I like red for a truck.

F. Write the following sentences. Add apostrophes where they are needed.

1. Dads new truck is parked in the alley.
2. Hes going to take our bikes to the beach in his truck.
3. Dad doesnt want to hurt the new truck.
4. Dad is careful when he opens the trucks door.
5. He hopes the truck wont get scratched or dented.

Grammar Practice 345

Index

A

A, an, and the, 248–249, 324
Abbreviations, 289
Actions, 18
    See also Verbs
Address, 16, 132, 133, 136, 289, 290, 342, 344
Adjectives
    in writing, 267, 332
    kinds, 262–263, 330
    placement in a sentence, 266
    that compare, 264–265, 331–332
    See also Antonyms; Describing words;
        Multiple-meaning words; Synonyms
Adverbs, 282–283, 340
Advertisements, 139
Alphabet
    cursive, 199
    manuscript, 195
Alphabetical order, 230, 314
And, but, and or, 239–240, 324
Announcements, 122
Antonyms, 74–75, 170, 171
Apostrophe
    in contractions, 292–293, 345
    with possessive nouns, 250, 292, 345
Article (of an encyclopedia), 317
Articles
    See *A, an,* and *the*
Audience, 109, 166–167, 182–189, 194
Author, 123, 301, 312

B

Body parts, 61
Book review, 123
Book parts, 312–315
    glossary, 314
    index, 315
    table of contents, 313
    title page, 312

C

Capital letters
    beginning of a sentence, 172, 197, 234, 284, 341–343
    days and months, 285, 341
    in abbreviations, 285–286, 342
    in an outline, 305
    in dialogue, 287, 343
    in greetings and closings, 287, 342
    pronoun *I*, 284, 341
    proper nouns, 284–287, 341–343

Captions, 131
Card catalog, 298
CD-ROM, 317
Character, 98, 129, 150
    See also Clusters; Story maps
Charts
    definition, 86
    FATP chart, 109
    5Ws chart, 110
    KWL chart, 87
Classroom objects, 40–41
Clothes, 70–71
Clusters
    character map, 89
    for prewriting, 110
    web, 88, 159
Colors, 20, 21
Comma
    in a compound sentence, 240, 291, 345
    in a series, 290
    in dialogue, 291, 345
    in letters, 290, 344
    to set off certain words, 290
    with large numbers, 290
Community, 56–59
Community workers, 58–59
Comparisons, 142, 264–265
Compound sentences, 240, 324
Compound subjects and predicates
    See **And, but,** and **or**
Compound words, 76–77
Computers
    CD-ROM, 317
    drafting, 113
    e-mail, 128
    in a library, 299
    Internet, 297, 299, 320–321
    publishing, 121
    saving ideas, 159
    spell check, 118–119
Conclusion, 309, 311
Conjunctions
    See **And, but,** and **or**
Contractions, 292–293, 345
    spelling *it's, they're, you're*, 224–225
Conversation
    See Discussion

D

Days of the week, 66, 285
Demonstrative pronouns
    See **This, that, these,** and **those**

Describing words
    colors, 20
    feelings, 19
    health, 60–61
    numbers, 44–47
    order words, 47
    shapes, 21
    sizes, 22
    smells, 24
    sounds, 23
    tastes, 26–27
    touch, 25
    See also Adjectives
Description
    as a purpose for writing, 162, 164
    of a person, 124
    of a place, 125, 162
    See also Describing words
Details, 93, 112, 122, 124, 127, 157, 304–305, 308, 311
    See also Adjectives; The Good Writer Guide
Diagrams
    for organizing details, 111
    in a report, 310
    in research, 303
    main idea diagram, 93
    parts diagram, 90
    process diagram, 91
    Venn diagram, 92
Dialogue
    in a play script, 145
    in writing, 177
    See also Capital letters; Punctuation
Diary
    See Journal entry
Dictionary, 230–231, 299
Directions
    as a command, 42–43
    for making something, 126
    to a place, 127
    See also Words that tell where
Discussion
    peer conference, 115
    talk and listen in a group, 188–189
Doctor's office, 60–61
Drafting
    See The Writing Process

E

Editing
    See The Writing Process
Editing marks
    See Proofreading marks
E-mail, 128
Encyclopedia, 297, 299, 316–317
End marks, 172, 288–289
    See also Exclamation point; Period; Question mark

Endings (added to words)
    -ed, *-ing*, *-er*, and *-est*, 220–221
    of plural nouns, 246–247, 325
    of verbs, 272–273, 336, 338
    suffixes, 78
Entry word, 170–171, 315
Envelope, 133
Exclamation point, 172, 236, 288, 344
Exclamations, 175, 236
Experts, 297, 318

F

Fable, 129
Fact, 138–139
Family, 32–33
Fantasy, 152–153
Feelings, 19
Fiction, 150–153
    See also Story
Food
    See Tastes
Formal language, 48–49, 166
Friendly letter, 132, 164

G

Glossary, 314
The Good Writer Guide, 158–179
    add details, 176
    choose good words, 168–169
    collect ideas, 158–159
    make sentences better, 172–175
    review your writing, 178–179
    save your writing, 178
    show, don't tell, 177
    think about your writing, 179
    use a thesaurus, 170–171
    write for a specific audience, 166–167
    write for a specific purpose, 160–165
Grammar Practice, 322–345
    adjectives, 330–332
    adverbs, 340
    capital letters, 341–343
    nouns, 325–326
    pronouns, 327–329
    punctuation, 344–345
    sentences, 322–324
    verbs, 333–339
Graphic organizers
    charts, 86–87, 109, 110
    clusters, 88–89, 110
    diagrams, 90–93
    graphs, 94–96
    KWL chart, 87
    story maps, 98–103
    time lines, 104–105
    webs, 88, 110, 159

Graphs, 94–96
    bar graph, 94
    line graph, 95
    pie graph, 96
Greetings and good-byes, 48–49
Guide words, 170–171, 231, 317

H

Handwriting
    cursive, 199–203
    how to hold pencil and paper, 194
    manuscript, 195–198
Health
    See Doctor's office
Homes, 28–31
Homonyms
    See Multiple-meaning words
Homophones
    See Sound-alike words

I

Ideas for writing and research, 108, 158–159, 296
Indenting, 140, 198, 202–203
Index, 315, 316
Informal language, 48–49, 167
Internet, 297, 299, 320–321
Interview, 318
Introduction
    introducing people, 51
    of a research report, 306–308, 310
Invitation, 134, 161

J

Jobs
    See Community workers; Doctor's office; School words
Journal entry, 130, 160, 165

K

Key words, 296, 315, 316, 320–321

L

Labels, 131
Letters (to people)
    capitalization and punctuation, 290, 342, 344
    e-mail, 128
    envelope, 133
    friendly letter, 132, 164
    invitation, 134, 161
    parts of a letter, 132
    postcard, 136
    thank-you note, 135, 163
Letters (of the alphabet)
    cursive, 199
    manuscript, 195
    See also Spelling
Library, 37, 297, 298–299
Limerick
    See Poems
List, 108, 137, 157, 158, 162, 296
Listening
    in a group, 189
    to a message, 185
    to a story, 183
    to a talk, 187
Location words, 56–57, 125

M

Magazine, 297, 299, 319
Main idea
    diagram, 93
    for a summary, 157
    in outlines, 304–305, 308–309
    in writing, 140, 306–309, 311
Map, 97, 127, 190, 191, 193
Margins, 198, 202–203
Messages
    e-mail, 128
    spoken, 184–185
    written, 137
Money, 45
Months of the year, 67, 285
Moral, 129
Multiple-meaning words, 80–81

N

Name, 16
    See also Nouns (proper)
Needs
    See Ask for help
Newsletter, 138–139
News story, 138
Notes
    during an interview, 318
    for a research report, 300–304
    for a summary, 157
    telephone message, 137
    thank-you note, 135, 163
Nouns
    common, 242–244, 325
    in writing, 251, 326
    plural, 246–247, 325
    possessive, 250, 326
    precise, 251, 326
    proper, 245, 325
    singular, 246–247

Numbers, 44–47, 195
    See also Time

O

Occupations
    See Community workers; Doctor's office; School words
Onomatopoeia, 149
Opinion, 139, 143
Order words, 47, 69, 141
Outline, 304–309

P

Paragraph
    in a research report, 308, 310
    opinion paragraph, 143
    sequence paragraph, 141
    that compares, 142
    with examples, 140
    writing in cursive, 202–203
    writing in manuscript, 198
Parts of speech
    See Adjectives; Adverbs; Nouns; Prepositions; Pronouns; Verbs
Peer conference, 115
Penmanship
    See Handwriting
Period
    as a decimal point, 289, 344
    in abbreviations, 289, 344
    in sentences, 172, 197, 234, 236, 288, 344
Personal narrative
    See Story (personal narrative)
Phone number, 16, 137
Pictures
    See Visuals
Play
    act, 145
    actor, 144
    playwright, 144
    scene, 145
    script, 145, 165
    stage, 144
    theater, 144
Plot, 150
    See also Story maps
Poems
    limerick, 148, 163
    rhyming poem, 146–147, 164, 165
    with sound words, 149
Portfolio for writing, 178–179
Postcard, 136, 287
Predicate, 238–239
Prefixes, 79, 323
Prepositions
    See Words that tell where
Prewriting
    See The Writing Process

Pronouns
    agreement, 261, 328
    in writing, 261, 329
    object, 258–259, 328
    possessive, 257
    subject, 252–256, 327
    this, *that*, *these*, *those*, 260, 329
Proofreading
    See The Writing Process
Proofreading marks, 117
Publisher, 312
Publishing
    See The Writing Process
Punctuation, 288–291, 344–345
    See also Apostrophe; Comma; End marks; Exclamation point; Grammar practice; Period; Question mark
Purpose for writing, 109, 160–163

Q

Question mark, 172, 235, 288, 344
Questions
    asking and answering, 50, 52–53
    for research, 296, 318
    writing, 175, 235, 288, 344
Quotation marks
    in dialogue, 291, 345
    to show exact words from a book, 302

R

Realistic fiction, 151
Reading aloud, 182
Research report, 306–311
    See also Research process
Research process
    choose a topic, 296
    find information, 297
    outline, 304–309
    research questions, 296, 300, 303, 304, 305
    take notes, 300–303
    write a research report, 306–311
Resources
    books, 297–301, 312–315
    dictionary, 230–231, 299
    encyclopedia, 316–317
    experts, 297, 318
    in a library, 298–299
    Internet, 297, 299, 304–305, 320–321
    magazines, 297, 299, 319
Reviewing your writing
    See The Good Writer Guide
Revising
    See The Writing Process
Revising marks, 116
Rhyme, 146–148
Roman numerals, 305, 307–308

S

Safety, 64–65
School words, 34–43
Seasons, 67
Sensory words
    definition, 125
    feelings, 19
    smells, 24
    sounds, 23
    tastes, 26–27
    touch, 25
Sentences
    combining, 173
    complete, 172, 238
    compound, 240, 324
    in writing, 172–175, 241
    negative, 237, 322
    predicate, 238–239, 323
    punctuation, 234–236
    run-on, 174
    subject, 238–239, 323
    types, 234–236, 322
Sequence, 47, 69, 141
Setting, 150, 151
    See also Story maps
Shapes, 21
Signs, 64–65
Sizes, 22
Smells, 24
Sounds, 23
    See also Onomatopoeia
Sound-alike words, 82–83, 224–225
Speaking
    ask for and give directions, 56–57
    ask for help, 52–53
    give a message, 184
    give a talk, 186
    greetings and good-byes, 48–49
    introduce people, 51
    peer conference, 115
    personal information, 16
    say *please* and *thank-you*, 50, 52
    talk in a group, 188
    tell time, 68–69
Spelling
    consonant sounds, 204–209
    frequently misspelled words, 226–227
    long vowels, 214–215
    long words, 223
    one sound with two letters, 211
    plurals, 222
    short vowel sounds, 210
    spelling tips, 228–229
    two sounds with two letters, 212–213
    use spell-check on a computer, 118–119
    vowel sounds, 218
    words that sound alike, 224–225
    words with *c* and *g*, 216
    words with *-ed, -ing, -er, -est*, 220–221
    words with vowel + *r*, 217
Statements, 175, 234
    See also Period; Punctuation; Sentences
Story
    fable, 129
    fantasy, 152–153
    fiction, 150
    parts of a story, 150
    personal narrative, 154–155, 165
    realistic fiction, 151
Story maps, 98–103
    beginning, middle, and end, 99
    cause-and-effect, 103
    character, setting, and plot, 98
    goal-and-outcome, 102
    problem-and-solution, 101
    sequence chain, 100
Subject (of a sentence), 238–239, 270–275, 323
Subject-verb agreement, 270–275
Suffixes, 78, 220–221
    See also Endings
Summary, 156–157
Synonyms, 72–73, 170–171

T

Table of contents, 313
Tastes, 26–27
Technology
    See Computers
Telephone number, 16, 137
Textures
    See Sensory words (touch)
Thank-you note, 135, 163
Thesaurus, 169–171
This*, *that*, *these*, and *those, 260, 309, 329
Time
    days, 66, 285
    months, 67, 285
    seasons, 67
    telling time, 68
    time-order words, 69, 141
Time lines, 104–105
Title
    of a book, 123, 287, 301, 312, 343
    of a magazine, 319
    of a person, 284, 343–344
    of a research report, 306, 310
Title page, 312
Topic
    choosing, 108–109, 296
    in a magazine, 319
    researching in an encyclopedia, 317
Topic sentence, 112, 125, 140, 141, 142, 307, 311
Transportation, 62–63
    See also Signs

U
Underlining book titles, 123, 301

V
Venn diagram, 92
Verbs
    action, 18, 268–269
    agreement, 272, 334–335, 338–339
    future tense, 276–277, 338
    has, *have*, 271, 333
    helping verbs, 278–280
    in writing (vivid words), 169, 281, 339
    linking, 270, 333, 338
    main, 278–280
    past tense, 273–275, 336–338
    present tense, 272, 336, 338
Visuals
    finding or making, 190, 303
    using, 182, 186, 191, 310–311
    viewing, 183, 187, 192–193
Vivid words, 169, 170, 281

Weather, 70–71
Web
    See Clusters
Web site, 321
    See also Computers; Internet
Word building
    compound words, 76–77
    prefixes, 79
    suffixes, 78
    See also Spelling
Word processing, 118–119, 121

Words about you, 16–33
Words that tell where, 56–57, 63, 125
World Wide Web, 320–321
    See also Computers; Internet
The Writing Process
    drafting, 112
    editing, 117
    prewriting, 108–111
    proofreading, 117
    publishing, 120
    revising, 114–116
    using the computer, 113, 118–119, 121
Writing, kinds of
    advertisement, 139
    announcement, 122
    book review, 123
    caption, 131
    description, 124–125, 162
    directions, 126–127
    e-mail, 128
    fable, 129
    invitation, 134, 161
    journal entry, 130, 165
    label, 131
    letter, 132–136, 164
    list, 108, 137, 157, 158, 162, 296
    message, 137
    news story, 138
    newsletter, 138–139
    note, 132–136
    paragraph, 140–143, 198, 202–203
    play, 144–145, 165
    poem, 146–149, 163, 164, 165
    report, 164, 310–311
    story, 129, 150–155, 165
    summary, 156–157
    thank-you note, 135, 163

Acknowledgments, continued

Batista Moon Studio: p297 and p316 (encyclopedias).

Bruce Coleman, Inc.: p71 (fall, © Barbara Williams), p136 (alligator, © John Shaw).

Cartesia: p3, p10 and p180 (map).

Corbis: (all © Corbis) p23 (noisy, © James L. Amos), p25 (smooth skin, © Barbara P. Williams), p25 (wet hair, © DigitalStock), p28 (house, © Lester Leftkowitz/Corbis Stock Market), p58 (farmer, © Ed Bock/Corbis Stock Market), p70 (summer, © Michael Keller/Corbis Stock Market), p75 (fast, © DigitalStock), p77 (rainbow, © DigitalStock; waterfall, ©Kevin R. Morris), p81 (train, © Alan Carey; jam, © DigitalStock), p82 (blue, © DigitalStock), p136 (Everglades, © David Muench), p141 (making salsa), p155 (Tokyo, © B.S.P.I.), p176 (soccer, © Tim Pannell/Corbis Stock Market), p193 (dog, © DigitalStock), p203 (Earth from moon, © DigitalStock), p205; p211 (fish, © DigitalStock), p208 (kiss, © DigitalStock), p210 (Ox, © Jack Fields), p211 (whale, © DigitalStock), p213 (frog and sky, © DigitalStock), p214 (sea, © DigitalStock; feet, © Jerry Tobias), p215 (boat, © DigitalStock), p216 (city, © DigitalStock), p217 (bird, © DigitalStock), p218 (moon, © DigitalStock), p297 and p299 (flowers, © DigitalStock).

Digital Studios: p41 (glue), p75 (empty and full), p76 (bathtub, flashlight, and backpack), p87 (notebook), p98, p150 and pp152-153 (book), p195 and p199 (pencil), p190 and p191 (computer), p205 and p210 (egg), p211 (bath), p213 (stamp), p246 (glass and dish), p299 (dictionary).

John Paul Endress: p206 (back), p209 (six and zero), p211 (match), p212 (old belt), p214 (cake and tie), p215 (fruit and tube), p216 (cot).

FoodPix: p74 (hot chocolate, ©Evan Sklar).

Getty Images, Inc.: (all © Getty Images, Inc.) p4 and p15 (open book, © Siede Preis/PhotoDisc), p31 (bathroom © Rob Melnychuk/PhotoDisc), p41 (pencil, pen, chalk, ruler, scissors, eraser, and crayon, © Artville), p45 (one dollar, five dollars, ten dollars, twenty dollars, penny, nickel, dime, and quarter, © Artville), p59 (judge, © Jeff Cadge/The Image Bank), p70 (rain, © Darrell Gulin/The Image Bank), p74 and p171 (elephant and mouse, © PhotoDisc), p74 (glass, © John A. Rizzo/PhotoDisc), p75 (day, © PhotoDisc; night, © Adrian Pope/Taxi; new, © Artville; old, © Christian Michaels/Taxi), p76 (baseball, © Artville), p77 (popcorn, © Artville; sailboat and mailbox, © PhotoDisc), p80 (bark, baseball bat, and bat, © PhotoDisc; bank, © Ryan McVay/PhotoDisc; riverbank, © Michael Busselle/Stone), p81 (leaves, © Michael Melford/The Image Bank), p82 (eight, © PhotoDisc; blew, © Terry Qing/Taxi), p83 (sail, © PhotoDisc; won, © Mike

Powell/Allsport Concepts), p142 (father and son, © Art Wolfe/The Image Bank), p154 (girl typing, © John Terence Turner/Taxi), p155 (Tokyo, © V.C.L./Taxi), p156 (corn and popcorn, © Artville; mother and daughter picking corn, © Paul Chesley/Stone), p159, p297, p299, and p317 (computer, © Duncan Smith/PhotoDisc), p167 (swimming lesson, © Tracy Frankel/The Image Bank), p204 (ball, © Artville; cat, © PhotoDisc), p205 (leaf, cuff, pig and hand © PhotoDisc; jar, © Artville), p206 (key, beak, heel, and map, © PhotoDisc; bell, © EyeWire Collection; lamp, © Janis Christie/PhotoDisc; drum, © Artville), p207 (net, knife, and pizza, © Artville; can, © C Squared Studios/PhotoDisc; cup, sign, and quilt, © PhotoDisc), p208 (wrist, seed, hat, and ten, © PhotoDisc; van and mitt, © Artville), p210 (apple and pin, © PhotoDisc; man, © EyeWire Collection; inch, © Artville), p211 (shell and thumb, © PhotoDisc; peach, © Artville; ring, © C Squared Studios/PhotoDisc), p212 (gift, hand, bank, and disk, © PhotoDisc; lamp, © Janis Christie/PhotoDisc; ant, © Paul Beard/PhotoDisc; nest, © Ryan McVay/PhotoDisc), p213 (truck, © Donovan Reese/PhotoDisc; flag, © PhotoDisc; drum, © Artville), p214 (sail and night, © PhotoDisc; bunny, © G.K. & Vikki Hart/PhotoDisc), p215 (rope, © Spike Mafford/PhotoDisc; toe, © Jack Hollinsworth/PhotoDisc), p216 (cup and cat, © PhotoDisc; rice, © Ryan McVay/PhotoDisc; gem, © Lawrence Lawry/PhotoDisc; cent and ginger, © Artville), p217 (horn, © C Squared Studios/PhotoDisc; chair, © Ryan McVay/PhotoDisc; tear, © Paul Dance/Stone; deer, © Jules Frazier/PhotoDisc; fern, © PhotoDisc), p218 (cent, © Artville; cloud and boy, © PhotoDisc; crown, © C Squared Studios/PhotoDisc), p219 (ball, © Artville; saw, © PhotoDisc), p222 (babies, puppy, and puppies, © PhotoDisc; glasses, © Artville), p246 (cat, © PhotoDisc; lunch, ©Artville), p281 (ice skater, © Lori Adamski Peek/Stone), p287 (train, © Digital Vision), p297 (expert, © David Barnes/Stone) p297 and p299 (bee, © Artville).

Image Club Graphics, Inc.: p204 (cab), p213 (clock), p217 (star), p218 (screw), p219 (salt), p222 (box).

Index Stock Imagery, Inc.: pp54-55 (city park, © James Blank), p59 (fireman, © Doug Mazell), p80 (bark, © Barry Winiker), p125 (garden, © Gay Bumgarner), p181 (kids in El Salvador, © Alyx Kellington), p283 (dinosaur, © Stewart Cohen), p287 (biplane, © Larry McManus).

Lonely Planet Images: p181 (El Salvador mountain, © Kraig Lieb; El Salvador statue, people, and fishing boats, © Charlotte Hindle).

Lunar Planetary Institute: p321 (moon).

MetaPhotos: p209 (wagon).

NASA: p191 (shuttle).

New Century Graphics: p3, p13, and p295 (book), p3, p13, and p295 (magnifying glass), p9, p107, and p121 (printer), p46 (buttons), p68 (clocks), p74 (shoe and box), p75 (clean and dirty), p96 (pens), p113 (computer), p126 (maracas, bottles, and beads), p130 (journal and crayon), p133 (stamp), p135 (Mancala), p136 and p287 (stamp), p158 (rainbow card), p158 (notebook), p159 (index cards and box, notebook), p169 (duffel bag), p172 (clock), p178 (Review Your Writing), p216 (gum).

Peter Arnold, Inc.: p213 and p215 (crow).

PhotoEdit, Inc.: p29 (townhouse, © David Young-Wolff), p39 (principal, © Michael Newman), p58 (dentist, © Bill Aron; cashier, © David Young-Wolff), p59 (waiter and police officer, © Rhoda Sidney), p81 (train, © Jeff Greenberg; kids taking turns, © David Young-Wolff), p83 (sale, © Robert Brenner), p124 (boys, © Myrleen Ferguson Cate), p144 (kids in line, © David Young-Wolff).

PictureQuest LLC: (all © PictureQuest LLC) p29 (mobile home, © Michael Dwyer/Stock Boston, Inc.), p132 (Chinese Dragon, © Allen Russell/Index Stock Imagery), p217 (bear, © Fransisco Erize/Bruce Coleman, Inc.), p221 (kids skipping, © IT Int'l/eStock Photography).

Stockbyte: p77, p213, and p222 (hairbrush), p77 (keyboard), p83 (father and son), p137 (ingredients), p171 (baby), p210 and p222 (pot), p213 (plant), p219 (launch), p246 (flower).

StockFood: p209 (fizz, © Eising Food Photography).

SuperStock, Inc.: p71 (winter), p83 (sun, © Larry Chiger).

Elizabeth Garza Williams: p3, pp10-11, and pp180-181 (speech), p5 (hello), p6 (boy writing), p8 (girl with notecard), p12 (kids), p14 (girl), pp14-15, p16, p72, pp84-85, pp106-107, p180, p232, and p294 (chalkboard), pp16-17 (Words About You), p18 (Actions), p19 (Feelings), p20 (Colors), p21 (Shapes), p22 (Sizes), p23 (whispering, girl plugging ears, and boy with trumpet), p24 (Smells), p25 (Touch), pp26-27 (Taste), p28 (girl), p29 (apartment), p30 (girl, kitchen, living room, and bedroom), p32 (boy), p33 (family and relatives), pp34-35 (Words About Your School), pp36-37 (Inside the School), p38 (teacher and students), p39 (librarian, nurse, custodian, and boy), p40 (In a Classroom), pp41-43 (Things to Do), p44 (counting buttons), p46 (girl with buttons), p47 (Number Order), p48 (Say Hello), p49 (Say Good-bye), p50 (Say Thank You), p51 (Meet New People), pp52-53 (Ask for Help), p54 (girl), p56 (kids), p58 (boy), pp60-61 (Doctor's Office), p62 (girl), pp64-65 (Signs and Safety), p69 (Telling Time), p70 (summer girl, spring boy, fall boy, and winter girl), p74 (up, down, stop, go, good, and bad), p75 (happy and sad), p76 (classroom and fingernail), p77 (sidewalk), p78 (Suffixes), p79 (Prefixes), p81 (jam, leave, and turn), p82 (hole, whole, and ate), p83 (one, write, and right), p84 (boy), p104 (boy), p106 (boy), p108, p109, and p111 (The Writing Process), p114 (piñata), p115 (Revise), p116 (girl eating), p130 (boy writing), p132 (girl writing), p133 (girl mailing), p134 (girl reading), p138 and 139 (kids gardening), p146 (Rainy Day), p170 (boy reading), p172 (kids talking), p175 (girl with bag), p179 (Think About Your Writing), p182 (Read Aloud), p183 (Listen to a Story), p184 (Give a Message), p185 (Get a Message), p188 (Talk in a Group), p189 (Listen in a Group), p190 (cutting pictures out, looking at dictionary), p191 (boy with chart), p194 (Handwriting and Spelling Guide), p204 (desk), p205 and p206 (gate), p210 (bus and up), p211 (chin), p213 (smell), p214, p222 and p246 (kite), p216 (go), p217 (turn), p221 (girl reading), p223 (girl), p232 (Grammar Made Graphic), p246 (box), p288 (girl reading), p294 and p302 (boy typing), p297 (library), p301 (boy with pencil), p307 and p311 (girl typing), p318 (Experts).

Illustrations:

All illustrations by Lynne Cravath unless otherwise noted.

All children's illustrations by Damon Swisher.

Cover illustration by Stephen Durke.

Rick Allen: pp152-153 (The Rabbit, The Coyote and the Big Rock); **Doug Bekke:** p198 (alligator); **Annie Bissett:** p90 (Oak Tree), p91 (Life of an Oak Tree), p97 (U.S. Map); **Peter Grosshauser:** p7 (The Fox and the Crow), pp56-57 (In Your Community), p57 (Words That Tell Where), pp62-63 (Transportation), p67 (Seasons), p98 (Anansi and Turtle), p100 (fox and The Fox and the Crow), p147 (Tommy background), p193 (pet store and library); **Robert Hynes:** p150 (Story and The Little Lost Whale); **Loretta Lustig:** p129 (The Ant and the Bird); **Paul Mirocha:** p190 (map), p296 (honey bees), p313 (bee); **Francisco Mora:** p102 (The Fox in the Moon); **Ilene Richard:** pp72-73 (Synonyms), p148 (Limerick), pp224-225 (Spell These Right!); **Roni Shepherd:** p99 (The Ants and the Grasshopper and flower border), p149 (Ears Hear), p220 (dinosaur eating and under palm tree); **Robbie Short:** pp298-299 (library); **Krystyna Stasiak:** p89 (Little Red Riding Hood); **Lane Yerkes:** p101 (It Could Always Be Worse).

English At Your Command!
Development Team

Editorial: Julie Cason, Roseann Erwin, Dawn Liseth, Sheron Long, Jacalyn Mahler, Stephen Newitt, C. M. Antoinette Nichols, Juan Quintana, Andrea Weiss, and Ink, Inc.

Design and Production: Mary Helen Aguirre-Greenwood, Sherry Corley, Jeri Gibson, Raymond Ortiz Godfrey, Raymond Hoffmeyer, Stephanie Rice, Augustine Rivera, Susan Scheuer, Curtis Spitler, Jonni Stains, Alicia Sternberg, Terry Taylor, Teri Wilson.

Permissions: Barbara Mathewson.